ISSUES THAT CONCERN YOU

Bullying and Hazing

Jill Hamilton, *Book Editor*

GREENHAVEN PRESS
A part of Gale, Cengage Learning

GALE
CENGAGE Learning

Detroit • New York • San Francisco • New Haven, Conn • Waterville, Maine • London

Christine Nasso, *Publisher*
Elizabeth Des Chenes, *Managing Editor*

© 2008 Greenhaven Press, a part of Gale, Cengage Learning

Gale and Greenhaven Press are registered trademarks used herein under license.

For more information, contact:
Greenhaven Press
27500 Drake Rd.
Farmington Hills, MI 48331-3535
Or you can visit our Internet site at gale.cengage.com

Cover image copyright Monkey Business Images, 2008. Used under license from Shutterstock.com

LIBRARY OF CONGRESS CATALOGING-IN-PUBLICATION DATA

Bullying and hazing / Jill Hamilton, book editor.
   p. cm. — (Issues that concern you)
 Includes bibliographical references and index.
  ISBN-13: 978-0-7377-4183-4 (hardcover) 1. Bullying. 2. Bullying in schools.
3. Cyberbullying. 4. Hazing. I. Hamilton, Jill.
  BF637.B85B846 2008
  302.3—dc22

                             2008019212

Printed in the United States of America
3 4 5 6 7 12 11 10 09

CONTENTS

The words *bullying* and *hazing* usually conjure up images of school-yard fights or fraternity hazing, but in recent years it is becoming apparent that bullying and hazing are not just for kids. The kinds of adult bad behavior that have been in the news make it apparent that it is all the more important for kids to work on handling these issues when they are young so that they do not end up following the poor examples set by some adults.

Workplace bullying is coming to the public's attention. A 2007 Zogby International poll found that one-third of workers, or 54 million Americans, say that they have experienced workplace bullying. Office bullying behavior includes yelling, cursing, sabotaging others' efforts, intimidating, and name-calling. Many workers who face such a bully do not end up taking any action because they fear losing their jobs. People who are bullied in the workplace suffer in ways that last beyond the bullying incident. Those who are bullied can have a rise in depression, heart attacks, and post-traumatic stress disorder.

On the hazing front, adult bad behavior has also been in the news. The most common groups for adult hazing to occur in are those in which people work together as a team for some common goal. Hazing has been reported among firefighters, police officers, professional sports players, and military members. There was a case in 2007 in which three Japanese sumo wrestlers and their stable master were arrested for beating a seventeen-year-old sumo wrestler to death. The beating was perceived as a way to toughen up the young man and get him ready for professional wrestling. Some experts on sumo wrestling say that this incident will not stop hazing in the sport, because for proponents of this kind of hazing, the problem was not the beating but rather that it went too far.

Also in the news was a case in which a former Los Angeles city firefighter was secretly fed dog food. During testimony for the case, it came out that firefighters regularly participated in such hazing activities, which they called "chairing." Chairing pranks included

What Bullying Is and How to Stop It

Jennifer Castle

In the following selection Jennifer Castle offers an overview of bullying. The piece covers what bullying is, who bullies are, and whom bullies like to target. There is also a section on "innocent bystanders," that is, people who stand by while a bully is in action. "Did you know," writes Castle, "that if one person watching a bullying situation says 'Stop it!' half the time the bully will stop?" Castle is the creator of *It's My Life*, a Web site for teens about teen life.

Bully. What does the word make you think of? For some people, it's that girl at school who always makes fun of them. For others, it's the biggest guy in the neighborhood who's always trying to beat them up or take their things. Sometimes "bully" means a whole group of kids, ganging up on someone else. No matter what situation or form it comes in, bullying can make you feel depressed, hurt, and alone. It can keep you from enjoying the activities and places that are part of your life.

Bullying happens everywhere, whether it's your town or Paris, France. It happens all the time, and it's happened since forever. Because it's so common many adults think bullying is just a normal part of growing up. You've probably heard parents or teachers

Jennifer Castle, "What Is Bullying?" *It's My Life*, 2005. Reproduced by permission.

The words *bullying* and *hazing* usually conjure up images of school-yard fights or fraternity hazing, but in recent years it is becoming apparent that bullying and hazing are not just for kids. The kinds of adult bad behavior that have been in the news make it apparent that it is all the more important for kids to work on handling these issues when they are young so that they do not end up following the poor examples set by some adults.

Workplace bullying is coming to the public's attention. A 2007 Zogby International poll found that one-third of workers, or 54 million Americans, say that they have experienced workplace bullying. Office bullying behavior includes yelling, cursing, sabotaging others' efforts, intimidating, and name-calling. Many workers who face such a bully do not end up taking any action because they fear losing their jobs. People who are bullied in the workplace suffer in ways that last beyond the bullying incident. Those who are bullied can have a rise in depression, heart attacks, and post-traumatic stress disorder.

On the hazing front, adult bad behavior has also been in the news. The most common groups for adult hazing to occur in are those in which people work together as a team for some common goal. Hazing has been reported among firefighters, police officers, professional sports players, and military members. There was a case in 2007 in which three Japanese sumo wrestlers and their stable master were arrested for beating a seventeen-year-old sumo wrestler to death. The beating was perceived as a way to toughen up the young man and get him ready for professional wrestling. Some experts on sumo wrestling say that this incident will not stop hazing in the sport, because for proponents of this kind of hazing, the problem was not the beating but rather that it went too far.

Also in the news was a case in which a former Los Angeles city firefighter was secretly fed dog food. During testimony for the case, it came out that firefighters regularly participated in such hazing activities, which they called "chairing." Chairing pranks included

Japanese stable master Tokitsukaze was dismissed by the Japan Sumo Association over the death of a junior wrestler during a hazing incident.

putting dead rats in firefighters' lockers or strapping colleagues to a chair and pouring hot sauce over them. In the trial, the dog food prank was deemed to be hazing, and the victim was awarded $1.43 million from the city.

Military hazing is also coming under scrutiny. Carol Burke's book *Camp All-American, Hanoi Jane, and the High and Tight* reveals some of the previous secret hazing rites in some parts of the military. Many of the rituals are similar to those in fraternity hazing, including depriving lower-ranking members of sleep or food, humiliating them, or feminizing them.

The rationale for such behavior is the belief that such extreme activities foster team building and make members stronger people. But, as such activities are getting more negative publicity, groups are finding (or being forced to find) new ways to achieve these goals. Many groups are discovering that alternatives such as rafting trips, paintball, and ropes courses may well be healthier and more effective ways of achieving trust and camaraderie.

The bad behavior of adults is just one of the issues related to bullying and hazing that students, teachers, and society at large face today. Authors in this anthology examine the causes and types of bullying and hazing and suggest solutions. In addition, the volume contains several appendixes to help the reader understand and explore the topic, including a thorough bibliography and a list of organizations to contact for further information. The appendix titled "What You Should Know About Bullying and Hazing" offers crucial facts about bullying and hazing and their impact on young people. The appendix "What You Should Do About Bullying and Hazing" offers tips to young people who may confront the problems of bullying and hazing in their own lives. With all these features, *Issues That Concern You: Bullying and Hazing* provides an excellent resource for everyone interested in this pressing issue.

What Bullying Is and How to Stop It

Jennifer Castle

In the following selection Jennifer Castle offers an overview of bullying. The piece covers what bullying is, who bullies are, and whom bullies like to target. There is also a section on "innocent bystanders," that is, people who stand by while a bully is in action. "Did you know," writes Castle, "that if one person watching a bullying situation says 'Stop it!' half the time the bully will stop?" Castle is the creator of *It's My Life*, a Web site for teens about teen life.

Bully. What does the word make you think of? For some people, it's that girl at school who always makes fun of them. For others, it's the biggest guy in the neighborhood who's always trying to beat them up or take their things. Sometimes "bully" means a whole group of kids, ganging up on someone else. No matter what situation or form it comes in, bullying can make you feel depressed, hurt, and alone. It can keep you from enjoying the activities and places that are part of your life.

Bullying happens everywhere, whether it's your town or Paris, France. It happens all the time, and it's happened since forever. Because it's so common many adults think bullying is just a normal part of growing up. You've probably heard parents or teachers

Jennifer Castle, "What Is Bullying?" *It's My Life*, 2005. Reproduced by permission.

saying things like. "Don't let it get to you" or "You just have to be tougher."

But why should something that can make a person so miserable have to be part of growing up? The answer is, it doesn't! Each and every one of us has the right to feel safe in our lives and good about ourselves. So IML [It's My Life] put together this guide to give you all the basics of dealing with bullies.

Different Kinds of Bullying

Let's start by looking at the different kinds of bullying:

Physical bullying means:
- Hitting, kicking, or pushing someone . . . or even just threatening to do it
- Stealing, hiding, or ruining someone's things
- Making someone do things he or she doesn't want to do

Verbal bullying means:
- Name-calling
- Teasing
- Insulting

Relationship bullying means:
- Refusing to talk to someone
- Spreading lies or rumors about someone
- Making someone do things he or she doesn't want to do

What do all these things have in common? They're examples of ways one person can make another person feel hurt, afraid, or uncomfortable. When these are done to someone more than once, and usually over and over again for a long period of time, that's bullying.

The reason why one kid would want to bully another kid is this: when you make someone feel bad, you gain power over him or her. Power makes people feel like they're better than another person, and then that makes them feel really good about themselves. Power also makes you stand out from the crowd. It's a way to get attention from other kids, and even from adults. . . .

The Levels of Bullying

Physical Bullying Verbal	Physical Bullying Nonverbal
• Expressing physical superiority • Blaming the victim for starting the conflict	• Making threatening gestures • Defacing property • Pushing/shoving • Taking small items from others

Level 1

Emotional Bullying Verbal	Emotional Bullying Nonverbal
• Insulting remarks • Calling names • Teasing about possessions, clothes, physical appearance	• Giving dirty looks • Holding nose or other insulting gestures

Social Bullying Verbal	Social Bullying Nonverbal
• Starting or spreading rumors • Teasing publicly about clothes, looks, relationship with boys/girls, etc.	• Ignoring someone and excluding them from a group

Level 2

Physical Bullying Verbal	Physical Bullying Nonverbal
• Threatening physical harm	• Damaging property • Stealing • Starting fights • Scratching or biting • Pushing, tripping, or causing a fall • Assaulting

Emotional Bullying Verbal	Emotional Bullying Nonverbal
• Insulting family • Harassing with phone calls • Insulting size, intelligence, athletic ability, race, color, religion, ethnicity, gender, disability, or sexual orientation	• Defacing school work or other personal property such as clothing, locker, or books

Social Bullying Verbal	Social Bullying Nonverbal
• Ostracizing using notes, instant messaging, e-mail • Posting slander in public places	• Playing mean tricks to embarrass someone

Level 3

Physical Bullying Verbal	Physical Bullying Nonverbal
• Making repeated or graphic threats • Practicing extortion such as taking lunch money • Threatening to keep someone silent: "If you tell, it will be a lot worse!"	• Destroying property • Setting fires • Exhibiting physical cruelty • Repeatedly acting in a violent, threatening manner • Assaulting with a weapon

Emotional Bullying Verbal	Emotional Bullying Nonverbal
• Harassing based on bias against race, color, religion, ethnicity, gender, diasbility, or sexual orientation	• Destroying personal property such as clothing, books, jewelry • Writing graffiti with bias against race, color, religion, ethnicity, gender, disability, or sexual orientation

Social Bullying Verbal	Social Bullying Nonverbal
• Enforcing total group exclusion against someone by threatening others if they don't comply	• Arranging public humiliation

Taken from: New Jersey Cares About Bullying. Office of Bias Crime Community Relations; Adapted from Atlantic Prevention Resources.

Who Is a Bully?

Wouldn't it be great to peek inside someone's head, reading his or her thoughts? Let's take a look inside a bully's head. It helps us understand why he or she acts the way [he or] she does, and also helps us know how to deal with it.

Bullies come in all shapes and sizes. Some are bigger or taller than everyone. Some get in trouble a lot. Some are popular kids who seem to "have it all," with lots of friends and good grades. But look inside their heads and you'll find one thing that they all have in common: Something or someone is making them feel insecure, so they're bullying to make themselves feel better.

Why People Bully

Remember, though, that everyone is different and lives with different experiences. If we looked even more inside a person's head, we'd probably find some extra reasons why he or she is acting like a bully:

- She's having problems in other parts of her life, like something going on in her family or struggling with school.
- He may not feel like he's getting enough attention from parents or teachers.
- She's watched her parents or older siblings get their way by being angry or pushing other people around.
- He's being bullied himself, maybe by another kid or a brother or sister . . . or even his own parents.
- Her parents have spoiled her or haven't taught her about not hurting others.
- He's getting exposed to a lot of violence in movies, TV, and video games.

What about the person who's always nice to you when he's alone, but will join in when his friends start teasing you? Well, as you probably know, peer pressure is a powerful thing. People like to do what their friends are doing. They might think they're just having fun and not even realize they're bullying someone.

Some people act like a bully for a year or two, and then grow out of it. It can also go the opposite way: some people are bullied when they're younger, and then once they're a little bigger and more confident, become a bully themselves. Some kids only act like a bully to one person, like they have their own personal punching bag.

Some bullies set out to hurt someone, with the goal of making him or her cry. Others don't even know that their behavior is doing so much damage. In fact, you may be a bully yourself and not know it! We'll talk more about that later.

So, wow. Lots of different types of bullies out there. The good news is that we can deal with all of them in the same way.

Whom Bullies Target

Do you feel like you have a big target on your forehead, or maybe a sign on your back that says "Bully Me!" You're not alone. People who do research about bullies found that roughly 25% (that's 1 out of 4) kids experience bullying.

What makes someone that "one" out of the four? Here are some possible reasons:

- He's a different size—smaller or bigger—than most of other kids their age.
- She falls into some type of "minority": African-American kids at a mostly white school, girls in a shop class that's crowded with boys, etc.
- There's something that makes him stand out, like a disability that makes him walk or talk differently, or even just his name.
- She gets anxious or upset very easily.
- He doesn't have any or many friends and is usually alone.
- She doesn't have a lot of confidence and doesn't seem like she'll stand up for herself.

Some kids get bullied as a result of a single thing that happened, like an embarrassing moment that took place in front of other people.

Sometimes There Is No Reason

You may even find yourself a bully target for no particular reason! Maybe the bully ran out of people to pick on, or you were in the wrong place at the wrong time when someone was feeling particularly mean.

Usually, once someone is singled out by a bully, other people will know that person is a target and start bullying her or him, too.

If you're a bully "target," you have something in common with famous people like Tom Cruise, Mel Gibson, Harrison Ford, and Michelle Pfeiffer. These celebrities have all talked about their own experiences with being bullied. It happens to the best of us! . . .

How to Handle Bullying

Bullying is a serious problem. It makes people feel lonely, unhappy, and afraid. It makes them feel like there must be something wrong with them. It even makes some kids not want to go to school or play outside. If extreme bullying goes on for a long time, it can lead to violent cases of revenge, like you may have seen in the news. Many people who are bullied a lot as kids grow up with low self-esteem and all sorts of other problems.

In other words, it's very important to deal with bullying and not let it ruin your life!

Okay, so there you are, and someone is bullying you. What do you do "in the moment"?

- Ignore the bully. Pretend you didn't hear him. Don't even look at him. Walk right past him if you can.

- Don't cry, get angry, or show that you're upset. That's the bully's goal. Don't give her the satisfaction. Even if you're feeling really hurt, don't let it show. You can talk about or write down your reactions later.

- Respond to the bully evenly and firmly. Example: "No." "That's what you think."

- If you can, turn a comment into a joke. Example: The bully says, "Stupid outfit!" You say: "Thanks! I'm glad you noticed."

- Turn and walk away, or run if you have to. Remove yourself from the situation. Go to a place where an adult is present.
- Remember that you are not the one with the problem. It's the bully who has the problem.
- If you're being called names or teased, try "The Fog Tank." Imagine that you're inside a huge fish tank filled with white fog. Then, imagine that the insults are swallowed up by the fog before they reach you. Nothing touches you. Practice by thinking of the worst things a bully can say to you, then letting the fog eat them up.

The Most Important Thing to Do

If you're being bullied again and again, there's one "Most Important Thing" you should do: Talk to an adult. This is so important, we'll say it again. Talk to an adult!

Start with your parents. It's not "tattling." It's asking the people who love you to give you help when you really need it. If the bullying happens at school, make sure your parents discuss it with a school official, not with the parents of the bully.

If you feel you can't tell your parents, or your parents don't give you the support you need, talk to another adult you trust: a teacher, principal, school counselor, or someone at your church or synagogue.

If you feel you can't talk to anyone, try writing a letter about what's happening. Keep a copy for yourself and give it to an adult you trust.

If you don't want to talk to someone alone, bring a friend, sibling, or parent. It especially helps to bring someone who has seen the bullying.

Make it clear to the adult that you are really upset by what's going on. This is especially true if the bullying is "verbal bullying." Many adults don't take verbal bullying seriously, but the truth is, this is the kind of bullying that can hurt the most.

If the bullying is physical or violent, you can ask the adult to whom you speak NOT to reveal your name.

Do NOT keep it inside. Do NOT plan revenge against the bully or take matters into your own hands.

Preventing Future Bullying

Now that you've spoken to someone about the problem, there are lots of things you can do to prevent future bullying.

- Don't walk alone. Travel with at least one other person whenever you can.

- Avoid places where bullying happens. Take a different route to and from school. Leave a little earlier or later to avoid the bully.

- Sit near the bus driver on the school bus or walk with a teacher to classes.

- Don't bring expensive things or money to school.

- Label your belongings with permanent marker in case they get stolen.

- Avoid unsupervised areas of the school and situations where you are by yourself. Make sure you're not alone in the locker room or bathroom.

- Act confident. Hold your head up, stand up straight, and make eye contact.

- Brainstorm bully comebacks ahead of time, and practice them in the mirror. That way you'll have them ready when you need them!

More Ways to Cope

Sometimes, a situation with one bully is settled, but then another bully comes along and takes his or her place. There are many things you can do to make sure that doesn't happen.

- Bullies are really good at making people think they deserve to be treated badly. That's absolutely wrong. Keep telling yourself that you're a great person who deserves respect and kindness from others.

- Learn to be proud of your differences. Why would you want to be like that bully anyway? Never be ashamed of an illness or disability. The sooner you feel okay with it, other people will too.

- Spend lots of time with your friends. If you don't have any real friends, work on making new ones by developing interests in social or physical activities.

- Keep a journal about bullying incidents and how they make you feel, as well as bullying that happens to other people. You can also fill a journal with positives: all the things you like about yourself, your plans for the future, etc.

If none of this helps and the bullying you're experiencing is making your life very difficult, talk to your parents about the possibility of changing schools. You and your family might feel like this is giving in, but in the end, it may be worth it to get on with your life and be happy.

"Innocent" Bystanders

In a bullying situation, there are usually bystanders, but they aren't exactly "innocent".

Bullying usually happens with other kids around, right? Having an "audience" is very important to a bully. She wants people to see what she's doing, and that she has power over the person she's bullying. It's usually because a bully wants a reputation for being tough or strong, or because she thinks it'll make her more popular.

So what about the people watching the bullying? Why are they letting it happen? Here are some possible reasons:

- The bully is someone other people look up to and want to hang out with.

People involved in the entertainment industry in Indonesia staged a protest against the bullying of children.

- They want to "side" with the bully because to do that makes them feel strong. Siding with the bully's victim, on the other hand, would make them feel weak.
- They're entertained by the bullying.
- They don't think speaking up will help.
- They're afraid that if they say something, the bully will turn on them.
- Watching the bullying is a way to bully "vicariously." This means that they feel like they're getting their frustrations out by hurting someone even though they're not doing the hurting, just watching the hurting.

Did you know that if one person watching a bullying situation says "Stop it!" half the time the bullying will stop? This can be hard to do, but it's important to try. When you stand by and do nothing, that's saying that bullying is okay with you. It makes you no better than the bully himself.

If You See Someone Getting Bulled

Here are some things you can do if you see someone getting bullied:

- Tell the bully to stop. Examples: "Cut it out!" "That's not funny!" "How'd you like it if someone did that to you?" Let the bully know that what he or she is doing is stupid and mean.
- If you feel like you can't speak up, walk away from the situation and tell the nearest adult. Get them to come help. This is not tattling!

If you see someone being bullied over and over again—whether that person is a friend, sibling, or classmate—you can make a big difference in helping to stop it:

- If your school has a bullying reporting program, like a hotline or "bully box," use it.
- Make sure the kid who's being bullied tells his parents, or a teacher. Offer to go with him if it will help.

- If she doesn't want to talk to anybody, offer to talk to someone on her behalf.
- Involve as many people as possible, including other friends or classmates, parents, teachers, school counselors, and even the principal.

Do NOT use violence against bullies or try to get revenge on your own. It's possible that by speaking up or helping someone, you've made the bully want to come after you. Be prepared for this, and hold your ground. You already have adult support on your side.

Try to Remember the Golden Rule:

Treat others the way you would like to be treated. Stand up for someone when he or she needs it, and when you need it, someone will stand up for you.

Are You a Bully?

Are you a bully and don't know it? Maybe you know you're a bully, but don't know how to change your ways? Never fear! Help is here!

How do you know if you are or have ever been a bully? Ask yourself these questions:

- Does it make you feel better to hurt other people or take their things?
- Are you bigger and stronger than other people your age? Do you sometimes use your size and strength to get your way?
- Have you been bullied by someone in the past and feel like you have to make up for it by doing the same thing to others?
- Do you avoid thinking about how other people might feel if you say or do hurtful things to them?

If you have bullied other people, think about why. Think about how or what you were feeling at the time. Think about how you felt afterwards.

How Can You Stop Being a Bully?

- Apologize to people you've bullied, and follow it up by being friendly to them. They may not trust you right away, but eventually they'll see that you're for real.

- If you're having a hard time feeling good about yourself, explore ways to boost your self-esteem. Pick up a new hobby, do volunteer work, or get involved with a sport.

- If you feel like you're having trouble controlling your feelings, especially anger, talk to a school counselor about it.

There are many reasons to kick the bully habit. Many bullies grow up into adults who bully their families, friends, and co-workers, causing all sorts of problems with relationships and careers. It's hard to think about the future when you're feeling something here and now, but take a moment to see how your behavior may be laying down some pretty negative groundwork.

TWO

Bullying Is a Symptom of a Larger Societal Problem

Lakshmi Chaudhry

> In the following selection, Lakshmi Chaudhry describes how bullying based on rank begins in school and continues into adulthood. Chaudhry notes that bullying behavior mirrors some of the baser elements of the adult world, such as television programs that encourage participants to humiliate each other. She notes that "rankism" stems from the way our brain associates aggression with status, but that we also have the ability to overcome that impulse. Chaudhry is a senior editor at *In These Times*.

A nine-year-old girl in England feels ugly and wants to kill herself because her schoolmates call her "Blackie." A legal assistant in Oregon is terrorized by an autocratic boss who screams obscenities in her face and refuses to give her time off for surgery. An 80-year-old man finds himself at the mercy of abusive nurses at a convalescent home. A teenager is molested by his parish priest.

Each of these are examples of what author Robert Fuller calls "rankism," which he defines as "discrimination or exploitation based on rank." All around us, he says, a powerful "somebody" is bullying a "nobody."

Lakshmi Chaudhry, "The Power of Mean," *In These Times*, November 29, 2006. Copyright © 2006 *In These Times*. Reproduced by permission of the publisher. www.inthesetimes.com.

Discrimination Based on Rank

In his latest book, *All Rise: Somebodies, Nobodies, and the Politics of Dignity*, Fuller explores how rankism offers a powerful opportunity to organize around social justice and equality. Given "the diminishing returns of identity-based politics," Fuller argues that the concept of rankism is more inclusive and appealing:

Someone can hold a high rank in one setting (for example, at home) and simultaneously be low on the totem pole in another (at work). Likewise we can feel powerful at one time and powerless at another, as when we . . . experience the loss of a job, a partner, or our health. As a result, most of us have been victims and perpetrators of discrimination based on rank.

Such dynamics offer the potential for identification that can be transformed, he writes, into a movement to create a dignitarian society where "the dignity of all people is honored and protected."

On its face, Fuller's thesis is hard to fault. We all know something about being victimized simply because we were on the wrong end of a power relationship. And isn't giving our common experience a name the first step toward raising consciousness of its insidious and destructive effects?

Yet Fuller's concept of rankism—which invokes our capacity for empathy as individual human beings—fails to address the darker side of our relationship to authority. Our everyday responses to abuses of power within the hierarchies that structure our lives, from the schoolyard to the workplace, are far more complex and muddied than Fuller acknowledges.

Bullies Gain Power and Popularity

Take, for example, the success of reality television, premised on the recognition that we nobodies enjoy seeing our fellow nobodies humiliated by a somebody. The popularity of Simon Cowell on "American Idol" or Donald Trump on "The Apprentice" reveals our willingness to accept, even relish, the cruelty of authority figures when it is targeted at others. We instinctively condone mean, bullying behavior as part and parcel of the exercise of legitimate power.

Learning to respect and accede to the power of mean starts early in life. It begins on the playground, where children learn quickly to use violence and fear to enhance their social status. In the June 2005 issue of *Scientific American Mind*, German researcher Mechthild Shafer described the typical elementary school bully: "Bullies are usually very dominant children who have learned early on that they can become the leader of a group by being aggressive. Their modus operandi is to humiliate a student who is physically or psychologically susceptible to rise to the top of the social order."

More depressing—and telling—is Schafer's finding that children become more supportive of cruelty over time. After six years,

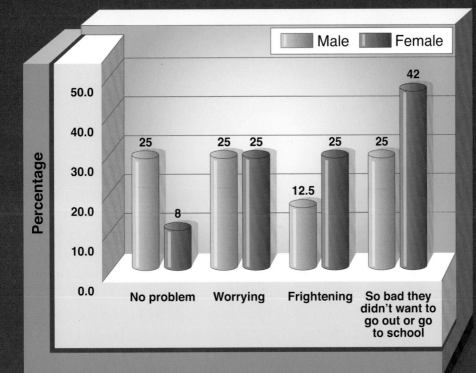

Kids on the Effects of Being Bullied

The Bullied: Effect on Students

Taken from: "A Report on Bullying," The Young Carers' Project, Dundee, 2002.

she writes, "In contrast to the bullies' relative lower standing during elementary school, they had actually become very popular with their classmates." Meanwhile, the victims "got few sympathy points. . . . Their peers acted as if they were not there or responded with outright rejection and whispered behind their backs. The bullies escalated this game, insulting and making fun of them. Many of the target children came to identify with the underdog role." The longer this went on, she notes, the more isolated the victims became.

The trend is no different in Canada, where psychologist Debra Pepler found 60 percent of the so-called "neutral" students were friends of the bullies, and half of the observers of bullying behaviors eventually became active participants and supporters. And UCLA psychologist Jaana Juvonen discovered that bullies were consistently among the most liked and respected kids among 2,000 sixth-graders in the Los Angeles area.

Bullying in Politics and the Workplace

Juvonen's research should hardly surprise liberals, for whom politics has come to resemble a bad high school flashback, especially under the aegis of the [George W.] Bush administration. Recent election years simply replayed the locker-room dynamic: Nasty Republican [GOP] operatives beat up on craven Democratic "pussies" for the benefit of an appreciative "objective" media, and an acquiescent American public, that seems more likely to punish the GOP for incompetence than its dirty tricks.

Kids will be kids, but as it turns out, so will adults—both in politics and in the workplace. Bullying is as common on the job as in the schoolyard. According to Bennett Tepper, a professor of managerial sciences at Georgia State University, 50 percent of workers say they've had an abusive boss at some point in their working career. Women may be more likely to be targets, but they are just as likely to be bullies.

Contrary to Fuller's claim that rankism is bad for the corporate bottom line, the research on its effects on employees shows that it may not hurt productivity. Like schoolchildren, workers are more likely to appease a bully than to confront him. "Many abused subordinates continue to perform at high levels," Tepper writes in an e-mail interview. "They do so because they believe that they have no choice (i.e., they have little mobility and believe that low performance will elicit further abuse or, possibly, termination)."

High performance may also be part of "an impression management strategy—trying to create a favorable impression in the mind of the abuser, thinking that doing so might deflect the supervisor's abuse toward someone else (another coworker perhaps)," says Tepper. And when faced with a flagrant abuse of power, a combination of fear, ambition and even schadenfreude makes other employees more likely to blame the victim than come to his aid.

Bullies Need an Audience

Worse, a bullying boss is likely to make her subordinates just as mean. Experiments conducted by Leigh Thompson, an organizational psychologist at Northwestern University, and Cameron Anderson, a business professor at the University of California, Berkeley, found that a middle-level manager is likely to reproduce the behavior of his punitive boss in order to please her, irrespective of his own temperament. "If the person in charge is high energy, aggressive, mean, the classic bully type," Thompson told the *New York Times*, "then over time, that's the way the No. 2 person begins to act."

Cruelty, then, is a communicable disease. Moreover, it requires the participation of the entire community, since the exercise of power—legitimate or otherwise—requires social recognition. While discussions of bullying tend to focus on the perpetrator and the victim, Juvonen notes that bullying requires the presence of an appreciative audience. The primary reward of bullying in schools is not so much the terror of the victim, but the opportunity for the bully to assert his higher social status in the larger community.

"Bullies would not bully someone without an audience," Juvonen says. "Even when these incidents of physical intimidation take place in the privacy of a bathroom, it's to ensure privacy from adults. But they know that rumors get around quickly about

Paul de Waard speaks to reporters after he and another man were shot trying to help a woman being attacked by a gunman. His fellow Good Samaritan died at the scene.

what so-and-so did to so-and-so, etc. So there is always an audience, whether visible or invisible."

All Rise simply sidesteps the psychosocial roots of rankism, resorting instead to social history. Fuller envisions a dignitarian movement that follows the arc of civil rights movements: People become conscious of injustice, recognize its "negative consequences" and then organize themselves into a movement for change.

Fighting Back

But, as he himself concedes, "When it comes to familiar varieties of discrimination, the victims and the victimizers are, for the most part, distinguishable and separate groups: black and white; female and male, gay and straight, and so on. The same thing that makes it easy to identify potential victims of these familiar isms . . . facilitates the formation of a solidarity group to confront the perpetrators."

However, he fails to recognize the enormous challenge this lack of identification poses for a dignitarian movement. While, a number of, say, African Americans may internalize racism or participate in a racist culture, their role can hardly be compared to the so-called "neutral" nobodies who actively enable the abuse of power within an organization or community.

Dividing the world into somebodies and nobodies does little to capture the complex dynamics of power within social groups. Unlike racism or homophobia, the underlying causes of rankism are rooted in the ancient hardwiring of our brain that associates aggression with status. It is why so many of us instinctively kowtow to our bullying boss, partner, peer, or even our president. In this, we are no different than our fellow primates.

Unlike chimps or gorillas, however, we do possess the ability to overcome our most primal impulse. "Is it natural?" Juvonen asks. "Yes. Is it inevitable? Absolutely not." Moral principles can indeed override the basic instinct for cruelty, but we first have to be willing to acknowledge the power of mean.

THREE

Social and Cultural Violence Is Causing Girls to Bully

Deborah Prothrow-Stith and Howard Spivak

In the following essay Deborah Prothrow-Stith and Howard Spivak note that girls are closing the achievement gap with boys in many ways and, tragically, violent behavior is no exception. In the past, girls would express their aggression through self-destructive behaviors such as running away or cutting. Now more girls are acting out with violence, fighting, and bullying. The authors blame social and cultural influences for the rise of violent girls. They cite movies featuring violent female heroines and a society that socializes girls to be more like boys as major factors in the rise of girls' violence. Troubled by the trend, they issue a warning: "Don't forget the girls!" Prothrow-Stith and Spivak are the authors of several books on youth violence, including *Sugar and Spice and No Longer Nice: How We Can Stop Girls' Violence*.

For more than 20 years, we have traveled throughout the United States addressing youth violence as a public health problem. We started hearing occasional stories about girls fighting some 15 years ago. Ten years ago the stories became more frequent; we started getting an earful about girls fighting.

Deborah Prothrow-Stith and Howard Spivak, "It's Not Only Guys Who Fight These Days," *The International Herald Tribune*, November 24, 2005. Reprinted with permission.

Turning to the numbers, our fears were confirmed. Not only were school personnel anecdotally reporting that girls were fighting more, but girls were also getting arrested for violent crimes at all-time increasingly higher rates as well. National data were beginning to show the increase.

There are those who discount the figures and explain away the changes in girls' behavior by saying, "It's about time they fight back," or "Girls' behavior hasn't changed, police are just arresting girls more," or just not believing that girls could do such things.

But why wouldn't girls' behavior change in this area, as in so many others? Statistics may not tell the whole story, but when coupled with real-life stories from throughout the country, the picture is clearer.

Violence among girls is on the rise.

In many areas, girls and women continue to close the gaps between their behaviors and achievement levels compared with that of boys and men. Tragically, violent behavior is no exception. As society has changed, the differences between the ways girls and boys display anger and aggression have as well.

Girls Are Fighting Other Girls

Today, American girls are showing their mean streaks. They are fighting, and not just in self-defense. They are fighting other girls. They are not yet fighting as much as boys, but the similarities are striking. Explanations of gender-based victimization only delay a focus on prevention.

Girls are different! In addition to the obvious biological differences, society socializes girls and boys differently. The gender inequality in America creates circumstances in which girls and young women are vulnerable to violent victimization in their families, intimate relationships and the larger community. We must take these differences into account. Girls must learn how to be non-victim and non-violent.

Girls are not different! Girls are clearly demonstrating their similarities with boys with increased participation in sports,

Bullying by Gender

	Percentage of Those Bullied	
Sex of Those Bullying	Boy victims	Girl victims
Only by boys	75.6	9.7
Mainly by boys	14.4	10.8
By both boys and girls	8.8	29.5
Mainly by girls	0.3	14.9
Only by girls	0.9	35.1

Taken from: P.K. Smith and Shu Shu, "What Good Schools Can Do About Bullying: Findings from a Survey in English Schools After a Decade of Research and Action." *Childhood*, vol. 7, no. 2, 2000.

enhanced academic accomplishments and expanded career achievements. When socialization and opportunity are coupled, girls' behavior has changed.

Two decades ago, psychologist Leonard Eron suggested that to prevent youth violence in America we should "socialize our boys more like we socialize our girls." We have done the opposite. We are socializing girls more like boys, and it is clear that girls are capable of similar levels of violence. Like boys, girls resort to fighting to prove a point, get respect, gain a reputation and for status.

Social and Cultural Influences Are the Problem

We believe that socialization and cultural changes explain the changes in girls' behavior.

Specifically, the entertainment media—movies, television, music, teen magazines—are depicting girls in roles a male superhero could play with hardly a script change. We are teaching girls, as we have for decades with boys, that fighting is appropriate and acceptable when dealing with hurt, pain, anger and conflict.

As we market violence to girls, the parameters around girls' behavior have changed and their repertoire of responses to problems and pain expands.

The major risk factors for violence include gun availability, poverty, alcohol and drug use, biological factors, witnessing/victimization, and social/cultural influences. Historically, these risk factors have lined up for girls no differently than for boys. The notable recent exception is the change in the social and cultural influences on girls.

Traditionally, high-risk girls acted out with self-destructive behavior (using alcohol or drugs, running away, suicide attempts, prostitution and cutting), not violence against others. Boys more typically externalized their risks with fighting, bullying, and violence. Now, violence and physical aggression are being marketed to our daughters in the same way as it has been to our sons.

Predictably, school is where much of this plays out. Students and faculty are reporting more hazing resulting in physical harm and illegal activity. We hear about girls being mean-spirited and aggressive toward other girls and more recently toward teachers. Standard responses consist of disbelief, uncertainty and expansion of "no tolerance" policies predicated on the threat of severe punishment—expulsion in particular—as the primary deterrent. But it is not working with girls, just as it hasn't worked with boys.

The problem rests in our "Rambo" hearts and "Terminator" minds. Equality is not the problem. Our values are. America has tolerated the epidemic of violence among boys for far too long. Maybe its spread to girls will wake us up to the impact of a toxic environment that is now affecting even the most resilient.

Are the changes in girls' behavior permanent? We really don't know. But we do believe in individual and collective action. We have experienced the consequences of delay and inaction. The change in girls' behavior is significant enough to issue this warning: Don't forget the girls!

FOUR

Schools Can Empower Kids to Stop Bullying

Dennis Murphy

> Dennis Murphy wrote the following article in the wake of the Columbine shootings. Murphy, the chief of the Springfield, Oregon, Department of Fire and Life Safety, has had previous experience with school violence. His department was the first to respond to a 1998 shooting at a local high school in which twenty-five students were wounded and two were killed. In the article, Murphy details the broad and long-term effects of bullying and offers ways for schools and students to prevent it. He lists strategies that have worked in curbing bullying, including setting up anonymous hotlines, encouraging antiviolence student organizations, and creating a school culture that does not tolerate bullying. Murphy notes that reports from students have stopped at least twenty-six threats of school violence. Murphy is the founder and board vice president of the Ribbon of Promise National Campaign to Prevent School Violence.

The bullying experience at school is nearly universal. As a child, nearly everyone experiences it at some level—spectator, bully, or victim. The experience is so common that many consider it just something that happens in almost every childhood and something to be largely dismissed as a serious threat. Yet, report after report

Dennis Murphy, "Preventing Bullying in Schools: Kid Power Is the Answer to Verbal, Physical Harassment," *Counseling Today*, vol. 47, September 2004, pp. 18–25. Reproduced by permission.

has documented the damage that cruel, long-term, and pervasive bullying can cause—physical and psychological harm, including depression, stress-related illnesses sometimes leading to suicide, and a desire to retaliate with violence.

A new economics report also links the destruction of self-esteem and resultant detrimental effects on educational and economic achievement. And the latest report from the Centers for Disease Control [CDC] indicates that high school students are increasingly likely to miss school because they felt too unsafe to attend. It therefore may come as a surprise that the solution to this problem is to be found among the kids themselves.

Bullying Has Big Consequences

A retrospective study during 14 years of a large group of high school students who suffered from low self-esteem and a resultant poor attitude was conducted by researchers from the University of Oregon's Department of Economics. The professional working paper demonstrates these students attain fewer years of post-secondary education relative to their high school cohort [group], are less likely to be employed 14 years after graduation, and, where working for pay, realize lower earnings. Further, the paper demonstrates that low self-esteem and poor attitude in high school are significant predictors of the degree of supervision under which individuals ultimately work.

While low self-esteem and poor attitude in students are not always the result of bullying, they are the most commonly reported consequences. These and other relationships included in the paper suggest that real educational and economic consequences of bullying have been previously ignored or at least underreported.

To examine changes in violence-related behaviors among high school students in the United States during 1991–2003, the CDC analyzed data from the national Youth Risk Behavior Survey. In 2003, one in three students reported involvement in a physical fight, and nearly one in ten reported being threatened or injured with a weapon on school property during the preceding 12 months. As a result, not going to school because of safety concerns increased significantly from 4.4 percent in 1993 to 5.4 percent in 2003.

The primary target for bullying prevention and safer-schools efforts should be the peer culture. The norms, actions, beliefs, and values within broad sectors of today's youth peer culture are socially destructive and demeaning.

Many youth experience a trial by fire in negotiating the complex and difficult social tasks involved in finding their place in this peer culture. Far too many fail this critical test, become lost within it, and wander aimlessly while seeking acceptance that is generally not forthcoming. They become homeless persons within the larger peer group, and their lack of fit is well-known among peers. This process forces many marginalized youth to affiliate with atypical or deviant peer groups, which can prove destructive to them.

Transforming this destructive peer culture is perhaps our most formidable task in the area of school safety. This culture is not of the schools' making, but schools are perhaps the only social institution, beyond the family, capable of addressing it effectively. Five ongoing strategies are recommended for your consideration in this regard.

Five Strategies to Stop Bullying

Strategy 1

Adopt and implement the Ribbon of Promise school violence prevention programs *By Kids 4 Kids* and *Not My Friends, Not My School*. These programs are designed to transform peer attitudes and beliefs about the risks to school safety that emerge from the peer culture. They promote ownership by peers of the tasks involved in preventing school tragedies and are highly recommended as a first strategy for enlisting the school's peer culture in this effort. These programs include a video that has been widely distributed and is available to all local schools.

Strategy 2

Bully-proof the school setting by adopting effective anti-bullying/harassment programs, such as 'STEPS TO RESPECT'. The best

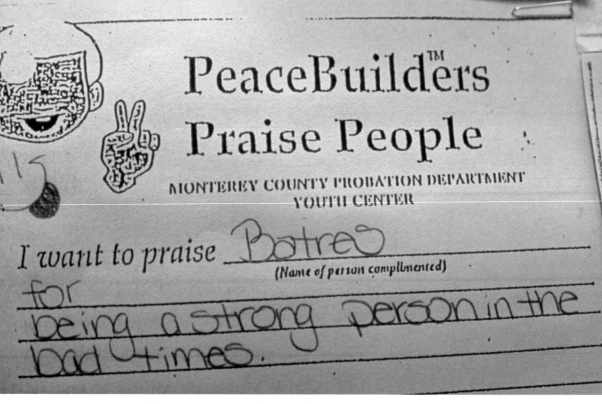

PeaceBuilders™ Praise People

MONTEREY COUNTY PROBATION DEPARTMENT
YOUTH CENTER

I want to praise ___Botres___
(Name of person complimented)

___for___
___being a strong person in the___
___bad times.___

Peace citations, that students give to one another from the PeaceBuilders program, reward students who change their negative behavior.

disinfectant for bullying, mean-spirited teasing, and harassment is sunlight. These events need to be defined as clearly unacceptable in the school by everyone (administrators, teachers, other school staff, students, and parents) and made public when they occur. Students should be given strategies for reporting and resisting them in an adaptive fashion, and the reporting of those who commit these acts should be made acceptable. The above-cited programs incorporate these principles and strategies.

Strategy 3

Teach anger management and conflict-resolution techniques as part of regular curricular content. The SECOND STEP violence prevention program, developed by the Committee for Children in Seattle, is one of the best means available for creating a positive peer culture of caring and civility and also for teaching specific strategies that work in controlling/managing anger and resolving conflicts without resorting to coercion or violence. This program was recently rated as the most effective of all those currently available for creating safe and positive schools by an expert panel of the Safe and Drug-Free Schools Division of the U.S. Department of Education.

Strategy 4

Refer troubled, agitated and depressed youth to counseling and mental health services and ensure that they receive the professional attention they need. Youth with serious mental health problems and disorders who are alienated, socially rejected, and taunted by peers can be dangerous to themselves and others. These students are often known to peers and staff in the school and should be given the appropriate professional and parental attention, access to services, and social supports. Having mental health problems combined with being the target of severe bullying and taunting by peers has proven to be a dangerous combination in the context of school shootings.

Strategy 5

Ask students to sign a pledge not to tease, bully, or put down others. Reports from schools that have tried this tactic indicate that it makes a difference in the number of incidents that occur and in the overall school climate.

Students Can Make a Difference

Kids have proven they can take responsibility for school safety. During a series of mass school violence in the 1990s, culminating in the attack on Columbine High School in Colorado, Ribbon of Promise founded a student organization known as *By Kids 4 Kids*. BK4K was founded on the principle that students were in the best position to learn in advance of threats of violence and weapons and to report them. To break a self-imposed code of silence, a 12-minute video was written, developed and acted entirely by students, with the assistance of a professional video production company. The video, called *Not My Friends, Not My School*,

What to Do If You See Bullying

- Don't ignore what happens.

- Let the person who is being bullied know you have seen what's going on and are concerned.

- Encourage them to tell someone.

- If it is in school and you are worried about it, you may need to report the incident. Try to find out who to report bullying to. If you are worried about putting yourself at risk, can you tell someone about the bullying in confidence? Write them a note about what you saw.

- Teachers are often the last to know that bullying is going on. If they are going to be able to do anything about it, they need to know it is happening.

- If there is a problem with bullying in your school you may want to encourage others to get involved in antibullying schemes such as poster campaigns or support groups run by pupils. Maybe you could put on a drama presentation to raise awareness in your school.

- Are you aware of your school's antibullying policy? Can you think of ways to make it more effective? You may be able to talk to your school council or members of the staff.

Taken from: "Bullying: Information for Secondary School Pupils," Childline, November 2007. www.childline.org.uk/pdfs/info-bullying-secondary.pdf.

emphasizes that students must speak up to protect their friends and their school. The video was distributed nationally.

Nationally prominent playwright William Mastrosimone created a play, known as *Bang Bang You're Dead*, designed to be performed by an all-student cast, that delivered a powerful message about the horror of school violence and the need to break the code of silence to report threats of violence. Since the premiere production, the play has been performed thousands of times around the nation and abroad and has received widespread acclaim in violence prevention.

In September 2002, the producers of Showtime Networks, Inc. announced the production of a made-for-television movie based on the play. The movie added a new and powerful dimension to the play by establishing a connection between bullying and violent school attacks. The movie was then aired several times before a national TV audience and was made available for schools through the Cable in the Classroom program.

So far, according to media reports, 26 threats of violent school attacks have been stopped by reports from students.

Anonymous Hotlines Help, Too

Students are encouraged to report threats of violence to someone they trust to keep their identity confidential. However, not all students will place their trust in another person. Students may fear harassment or physical retaliation for reporting. In some areas, regional or statewide 24-hour hotlines have been established to permit anonymous reporting. For hotlines to be used properly, a significant publicity campaign is required as well as prominent listing of a toll-free number (for example, on student identification cards and phonebooks).

Stopping bullying will require a paradigm shift in the student culture. Adults have successfully learned not to tolerate racism, sexual harassment, domestic violence, and other forms of intimidation. Students can learn to do the same with bullying. They must take the same initiative with bullying as they have in stopping school attacks. Only then will there be a serious reduction in the incidence of school bullying.

FIVE

Schools Do Not Do Enough to Stop Bullying

Juliette Hughes

In the following essay Juliette Hughes, a writer and teacher in Melbourne, Australia, argues that schools do not try hard enough to curb bullying. She writes from personal experience. Hughes relates an incident when two popular girls from prominent families tried to keep an overweight girl from joining the choir, citing a made-up "size rule." Hughes, the choir teacher, expelled the girls from the choir, only to have the school suggest that she reinstate them. "That was no surprise," she writes. "Over the years as student and teacher I had often seen teachers colluding with bullies to keep order." Hughes notes that schools need to do more than just create antibullying policies—they need to follow them as well.

In the '90s I taught singing at a large state secondary school. I'd been there a few years when something strange happened at a parent-teacher night: a woman came up to me and pressed a note into my hand. "Please," she whispered. "Please read." English wasn't her first language. I opened the letter and read it while she was there. It begged me to allow her daughter, a year 9 student, into my choir.

Juliette Hughes, "Whatever Schools Say, Bullying Still Flourishes," *The Age*, April 16, 2007. Reproduced by permission.

"She loves so much to sing," said the woman. "Please let her join."

"But of course she can join," I said, mystified. "The choir is open to everyone."

I'd started a choir, but kids need confidence to sing out. To encourage students to let go their shyness, I instituted a no-bullying policy. I had two rules that were set out clearly and repeated every time there was someone new. The students knew them so well that they would recite them to any newbies. The first was that every student had a right to feel safe and accepted there. (The second rule was "don't waste our choir-time with chatter" but the first one was, I always emphasised, the important one.) I also said that it was the zero-tolerance rule; that anyone breaking it was out of the choir forever. That should do it, I thought.

"Is she new here?"

"She here from year 7," said the mother. "She is big, yes, but maybe she can stand at back, please."

I still didn't get it. Big? What did big have to do with it?

"You know, the size rule."

It turned out that two of my best singers, both accomplished young girls from middle-class backgrounds, had been telling their classmate for two years that she was too fat to join the choir—that there was a "size rule". I reassured the woman that her daughter was in. Then I went and informed the music co-ordinator that the girls responsible for this situation must leave the choir.

Schools Do Not Support Teachers

Then the trouble began. A week later the music co-ordinator, a kind and decent man, told me that he had been asked to ask me to reinstate the two bullies. I refused. He supported me though he was under some pressure: the girls were popular, powerful and talented, with influential parents. But he knew as well as I that reinstating them would destroy the choir's anti-bullying policy: no student should trust it ever again. What if they apologise, I was asked. I replied that it had gone too far: they'd sat in that room for two years reciting the rule while cruelly flouting it and knowing the clearly stated consequence of doing that very thing. If they returned, it meant that the rule was void.

Bullying by Grade Level

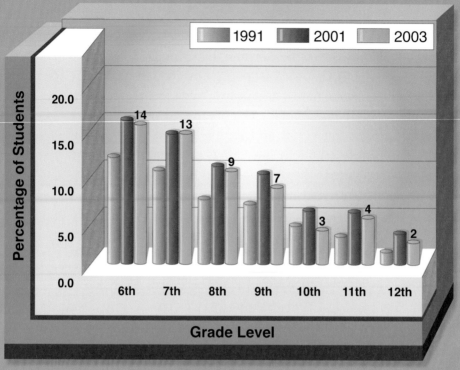

Taken from: U.S. Department of Justice, Bureau of Justice Statistics, School Crime Supplement (SCS) to the National Crime Victimization Survey.

There were repercussions: the targeted girl received threatening phone calls from cronies of the bullies; her house, which was close to the school, was graffitied and toilet-papered. Nothing was done about it. The pastoral care co-ordinator declared the targeted girl to be a "drama queen" for reporting the matter. Happily, the girl became a valuable long-serving choir member.

At the time, the school was going through an embarrassing period: it was dealing with a couple of lawsuits from past students who had been damaged psychologically and physically by bullying that had occurred in front of teachers who did nothing to stop it. The administration wasn't learning much from this. The school's official response to the continuing victimisation of that girl was also to do nothing.

That was no surprise. Over the years as student and teacher I had often seen teachers colluding with bullies to keep order. Again and again I'd hear the weasel words "S/he gives as good as s/he gets". Time after time, as student and teacher, I had seen kids punished when they tried to defend themselves after repeated abuse that was committed with impunity. I had seen bully-targets going through the official channels, but with little if any change to school culture that enabled the bullying. I had moved my own kids from schools where they were being bullied, schools that had proudly proclaimed their "anti-bullying" policies. They were usually right there next to the flatulent mission statements in the school handbook.

Bullying for school-age children often takes place on the school bus, where disciplining can be difficult due to a lack of supervision.

Bullying Can Happen at Any School

The recent scandal over the bullying allegedly caught on mobile camera at Xavier College seems to surprise some people [A video was distributed showing students at the elite private school beating up a classmate]: This is after all a prominent private school noted for its religious affiliations. But those who are surprised forget one crucial thing: despite its expensive amenities and spiritual values, Xavier is in the end still a school, and schools are hog-heaven for bullies.

Whether state or private, co-ed or single-sex, high-flying academic or educationally basic, whether sporty, arty or sciencey, schools have anti-bullying policies—and bullies. And bullies still bully, usually without sanctions. The ones who deny this are typically either bullies or their colluders.

In 30 years of teaching I rarely saw bullies and abusers confronted. But on one glorious occasion as a schoolgirl I witnessed justice as my headmistress (a wonderful brave Brigidine sister) scolded and sacked a male teacher who had molested a year 10 girl. Trembling, ashamed, she had been brought to Mother Basil by her friends to tell her story. She trusted the one whose job it was to protect her, and was believed, respected and vindicated. I wish that all victims had such champions.

SIX

Homophobic Bullying Is Bad for Everyone

Gerald Walton

> In the following essay Gerald Walton argues that homophobic bullying is a pervasive problem in schools. Still, he writes, "few school trustees and administrators have the courage to name it and implement policies and programs to curb it." Homophobic bullying affects everyone, regardless of his or her sexual orientation. He notes that homophobia is a powerful method of social control. The fear of appearing gay, and thus being subject to ridicule, affects how men and women dress, behave, and present themselves to their classmates. Walton teaches in the Faculty of Education at Simon Fraser University in British Columbia, Canada.

Have you ever been called a sissy, fag, dyke, lez, 'mo or queer? Have you ever called someone a sissy, fag, dyke, lez, 'mo or queer?

Used as weapons, these are mean and violent words that are commonly used to demean, diminish and humiliate others. Adults use such epithets as a way of exacting power over others both in real life and in popular culture such as music, movies and television shows. Similarly, kids employ such slurs during schoolyard bullying.

"That's so gay" has become an expression of anything deemed undesirable, and "Don't be a homo" serves to caution youth not to be seen as anything other than heterosexual.

These are expressions of homophobia. In general, homophobia is a prejudicial attitude against gays and lesbians, expressed as discrimination or verbal and physical violence.

The most vicious form of homophobia is gay-bashing. In 2001, Aaron Webster was clubbed, kicked and stomped to death by a group of four young men in [Vancouver's] Stanley Park. In 1998 in Wyoming, 22-year-old student Matthew Shepard was tortured and beaten to death by two young men. They were both targeted and murdered because they were gay. Scores of others worldwide have met similar, horrible deaths. Families and loved ones are left in the wake of grief to grapple with the impact of this homicidal form of homophobia.

Schools Are Not Doing Enough to Stop Homophobic Bullying

Homophobic bullying is a routine form of violence in schools. Still, few school trustees and administrators have the courage to name it and implement policies and programs to curb it. Research from Canada, the United States, Britain, Australia, Israel and other countries has demonstrated concretely that lesbian, gay,

Gay Teens More Likely to Be Bullied

• Lesbian or gay participants were three times as likely as heterosexual youth to report having been bullied.

• In contrast, lesbian or gay youth were about 80 percent less likely than heterosexuals to say they had bullied someone.

Taken from: Society for Adolescent Medicine Annual Meeting, Denver, March 28–31. News release, Children's Hospital Boston.

Marking International Day for Victims of Torture, activists claim homophobia as one of the causes of abuse.

bisexual, and transgender (LGBT) youth feel unsafe in their schools. For many LGBT youth, self-worth and academic achievement suffer. LGBT youth tend to have higher rates of isolation, depression, and suicidal ideation than do other students.

Though violence against LGBT people is real and pervasive, homophobic violence is not directed only towards LGBT people. Heterosexuals also become targets. Azmi Jubran, a straight man, as a high school student in North Vancouver suffered the effects of unchecked and escalated homophobic violence. Instead of dropping out of school, Jubran filed a human rights complaint against the North Vancouver school district for failing to provide protection from this form of violence. The case went through the court system and the Supreme Court of Canada (ruling against the school district) finally affirmed that school districts are obligated to provide safe learning environments free of harassment. If the district had taken a leadership role in this respect, perhaps this violence and exorbitant legal costs could have been avoided.

Sadly, Hamed Nastoh cannot provide an account of his own similar story. Nastoh was also identified as straight, but in 2000 he jumped off [Vancouver's] Pattullo Bridge as a result of the unrelenting torments he faced at school. Since then, Nastoh's mother has become an advocate of anti-bullying initiatives in schools, including anti-homophobia.

Homophobia Affects Everyone

In addition to motivating violence, homophobia strongly influences how we act, communicate and function in the world. Consider how males are taught from boyhood to suppress feelings, to "tough it up." Appearing masculine is equated with being straight. Boys generally learn to posture themselves as tough and masculine so they are not perceived to be gay. People tend to perceive feminine characteristics in boys as a problem to be corrected. For boys and men, homophobia is a powerful agent of social control.

Similarly, consider how females are taught to be "proper" girls and women. Girls are generally taught to behave in ways that are both feminine and submissive; it is generally unacceptable for girls or women to act aggressively, except perhaps in sports.

Otherwise, aggressive girls and women are often perceived to be tomboys and lesbians. Masculine women, regardless of sexual orientation, are assumed to be lesbians. For girls and women, homophobia is a powerful agent of social control that imposes social expectations of femininity and submission.

Homophobia adversely influences the lives of all of us, regardless of our sexual orientation. That is why May 17, International Day Against Homophobia [a holiday started in Canada in 2003 to celebrate the homosexual experience], matters to everyone.

SEVEN

Cyberbullying Is a Serious Problem

Helen A.S. Popkin

Helen A.S. Popkin wrote the following article in response to a study on teens and cyberbullying that found that about a third of teenagers who use the Internet report being targets of "annoying and potentially menacing online activities." Popkin feels that adults, who may engage in a bit of their own cyberbullying at the workplace, tend to dismiss the problem, thinking it is not that serious and that teenagers can handle situations on their own. The problem with this attitude, she argues, is that teenagers are not always capable of making sensible decisions. She also notes that cyberbullying often turns into real world harassment. Popkin is a regular contributor to MSNBC.com.

Teenagers can be serious jerks. You don't need research by the Pew Internet and American Life Project on cyberbullying to know that. It's interesting to note however, that at the dawn of the 21st century, teenagers have effectively transferred their jerk skills from corporeal [physical] to virtual, launching torments once reserved for the lunchroom, school hallway and bus stop into cyberspace.

According to Pew's recently released study, "About one third (32 percent) of all teenagers who use the Internet say they have been targets of a range of annoying and potentially menacing online activities." These youthful indiscretions include threatening messages, private online conversations shared with others and embarrassing photos and rumors posted for all the world to forward.

This is ugly, wiggle-head inducing information. Granted, a bus stop beat down is recognizably and immediately more damaging than an acronym-rich text threat. And the research also showed that 67 percent of teens surveyed said they're more likely to be bullied or harassed offline. But there's a gap in information here, one that arguably encourages the casual reader to summarize something along the lines of, "Hey, this cyberbullying isn't nearly as bad as we expected. No big deal, really."

That's certainly the opinion of one delightful 15-year-old boy surveyed. According to this charming young lad, he once threatened to kill someone online, but hey "I played a prank on someone. It wasn't serious." So why not take the kids at their word—they're generally pretty good at navigating those moral gray areas, right? It's not like they ever do dumbass stuff like stick a firecracker up a frog's rectum and light it. Or knock up their middle school teacher. Or run away with some 32-year-old dude they met on MySpace.

Except, oh wait . . . they do. Because they're teenagers. Their brains haven't finished cooking. Though it can be said of some adults (like the ones who get Pearl Jam tattoos), kids don't comprehend the Long Haul. As near as I can tell, the Pew study does not budget for the teenage brain. Most kids, like the jocular young man with the death threat mentioned earlier, don't comprehend the things that do damage if that damage can't be seen by the naked eye.

Cyberbullying Leads to Real-World Bullying

Let's face it. Once a social issue makes it as plot point on "Law & Order," we better start getting concerned. Now, if you're like me, all the "L&O" franchises start to run together. But I do recall an episode where this popular high school girl got killed by this

The Most Common Types of Cyberbullying

Making Private Information Public Is the Most Common Form of Cyberbullying		
Have you, personally, ever experienced any of the following things online?	**Percentage of Student Responses**	
	Yes	**No**
Someone taking a private e-mail, IM, or text message you sent them and forwarding it to someone else or posting it where others could see it	15	85
Someone spreading a rumor about you online	13	87
Someone sending you a threatening or aggressive e-mail, IM, or text message	13	87
Someone posting an embarrassing picture of you online without your permission	6	94
Answered "yes" to any of the four previous questions	32	68

Taken from: Pew Internet and American Life Project Parents and Teen Survey, October–November 2006.

fat chick's brother because she took cell phone pictures of the fat chick naked in the locker room and then e-mailed it to everyone or posted it on the InterWeb or whatever.

Fat Chick ended up shooting and killing Dead Popular Chick's BFF for hanging a pig fetus on her locker. Or something like that. I don't really remember. But it doesn't matter. What I mean to say is this: Where is the Pew research on the connection between cyberbullying and real world harassment? Because it happens, and not just on "Law & Order."

Let's talk Brooks Brown. That's the kid Columbine psychopath Eric Harris posted death threats about but later spared the day of the 1999 school massacre. Brown's parents reported the Internet death threat to police, along with online information hinting at the fact that Harris was building bombs. As is well documented, the police did not follow up.

Tina Meier displays photos of her daughter, Megan, who hung herself after receiving cruel messages on MySpace.

That's an extreme case, and perhaps even tasteless to cite following a description of a particularly exploitive "Law & Order" episode. It's also the most profound example of what happens when adults miscalculate the connection between cyber and real-world bullying. In fact, adults remained grossly inaccurate even after the fact, launching an anti-bullying crusade when the point was horribly moot.

Such misguided hysteria can be damaging, leading to the persecution of every kid venting his or her teenage angst online. And I'm sure not advocating that. But there's a fine line between overreacting and brushing off the issue altogether.

Adults Do It Too

Maybe grown-ups want to believe cyberbullying ain't so bad because, to varying degrees, many adults indulge in it as well. Internet anonymity grants the freedom to trash someone's chat room opinion on politics without the fear of facing them two cubicles over the next morning. Even in the office, it allows the meek and miserable to aggressively address co-workers via cap-infused e-mails lousy with exclamation points (albeit creating permanent records they may live to regret).

Lest we continue to downplay the implications of Internet bullying for kids or adults, consider Kathy Sierra. Earlier this year [2007], the software programmer who ran the site Creating Passionate Users closed her blog after suffering an onslaught of abuse—everything from childish insults to threats of sexual and physical violence. This harassment was not limited to Sierra's blog, but infected all areas of cyberspace with items such as a manipulated photo of Sierra with her throat cut as well as the posting of her home address.

The Sierra controversy led to an InterWeb blogger smackdown with all the most popular Web geeks arguing the implications and/or veracity of Sierra's experience. The fact remains that the Internet is full of evil nasty trolls, and they're not always harmless, no matter their age.

EIGHT

Adults Need to Protect Children from Cyberbullying

Dan Fox

> In the following selection Dan Fox describes the rise of cyberbullying. He reports that one-third of teens who use the Internet say they have been the target of cyberbullying and warns adults that they need to work to stop the problem. He notes it can be difficult for adults to find out whether cyberbullying is happening since kids often do not want to talk about bullying or admit to being bullied. Fox offers suggestions for concerned adults, such as getting involved in school policy decisions and monitoring Internet use. Fox is the executive director of Family and Children First, an organization that provides counseling and education for children and families.

School is back in session, and we all want our children to travel to and from school and learn in an environment that is free from violence and fear. For far too many children, that is not the reality.

Thirty-two children died as a result of violent events on school campuses last school year [2006–2007].

Each school year, 800 school-age children die and 152,000 are injured as they travel to and from school, the vast majority while riding in a family car.

Dan Fox, "Adults Must Join to Stop 'Cyberbullying,'" *The Courier-Journal*, October 1, 2007. Reproduced by permission of the author.

More than 5.7 million youths are involved in bullying incidents—as victim, perpetrator or both. A June 2007 Pew/Internet survey found that about a third of teens who use the Internet say they've been the target of "cyberbullying," with girls being more likely targets than boys.

There are many steps we can take to reduce the risks of violence in our schools and improve school transportation safety,

Where Cyberbullying Happens

The primary locations in (or mediums through) which cyberbullying victimization occurs are chat rooms (55.6 percent), via instant message (48.9 percent), and via e-mail (28.0 percent).

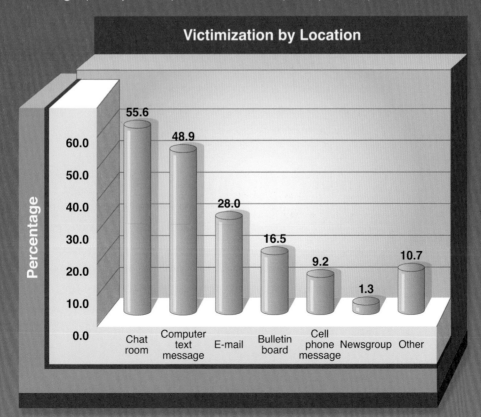

Taken from: J.W. Patchin and S. Hinduja, *Bullies Move Beyond the Schoolyard: Youth Violence and Juvenile Justice*, vol. 4, no. 2, pp. 148–169, 2006.

and they're worth reviewing at the beginning of every school year. But . . . while school violence and school bus crashes tend to grip our attention, it's far more likely that a bully will be the source of day-to-day fear for school-aged children. And as caring adults, it's our job to intervene.

A New Kind of Bullying

Bullying has always been around. Many adults today probably can remember when they or a schoolmate was shoved, shouted at or otherwise intimidated by another student. Bullying reached new heights early this decade [2000–2009], and schools, parents, the private sector and government agencies responded in force. But without a similar response, the exponential growth of e-mail, instant messaging and other electronic communication promise another massive escalation of bullying—this time in cyberspace.

Although the scene of cyberbullying may be virtual, the effect is still very real and potentially very damaging. And the longer bullying continues, and the later in a child's school years it occurs, the more likely its victims will experience depression or anxiety disorders, and turn to threatening, violent or other destructive behavior themselves.

Cyberspace Is Not All Bad

Without a doubt, the online social network is important to kids today—and it can be to their great benefit. Online communication helps kids reinforce friendships they make at school, allows them to discuss homework assignments and enables them to express their individuality by posting personal profiles (keeping them accessible only to identified friends, of course).

Nonetheless, the anonymity of cyberspace can foster bully behavior. Approximately 15 percent of teens in a 2007 Pew/Internet study reported having a private message forwarded or publicly posted without their knowledge, and 13 percent said someone had spread a rumor about them online. These incidents ranged from relatively benign to fairly exasperating. But 13 percent of teens in the study said they'd received electronic messages that were very aggressive or downright threatening, and those situations can be truly scary.

Von Steuben High School assistant principal Phyllis Hodges promotes a computer threat-assessment program in an effort to prevent school violence.

THE RELEVANCE OF THREATS TO FUTURE
BEHAVIOR IS WIDELY MISUNDERSTOOD

"I am going to kill you!"
To learn more about these words
Click here

Adults Need to Help

As parents, teachers, community leaders and trusted adult friends of children, we all can help kids deal with the sometimes intimidating issues, even if the kids with whom we interact won't outright admit to being bullied. As involved, caring adults, we can:

Monitor our children's Internet and texting behavior and intervene when we see an incidence of bullying—whether it's teasing, ostracism or physical threats.

Use these incidences and media stories about bullying as opportunities to talk with children about the topic, reinforce the value of each individual and reiterate that basic human kindness is as important in cyberspace as it is face-to-face.

Seek to learn about children's environment. Ask questions, such as: What's it like when you're in the cafeteria? Have you heard of kids at your school being bullied? Do you feel like e-mail and instant messaging make it easier to be unkind or cruel than when kids are talking face-to-face?

Intervene and show support for a child who has been bullied, and try to talk with him or her about the situation. Empathize with what he or she is going through and, in non-threatening situations, walk through a couple of positive response scenarios.

If our instincts tell us the incident is serious, it's probably better to get in touch with school or other authorities than to contact the families of other involved children ourselves. Let the principal or counselor know that we want the bullying stopped, and that we'll cooperate with them to find a solution.

Involve ourselves in neighborhood schools and ask direct questions about the safety measures the school employs. And encourage and support school efforts to educate students about what bullying is, how it can result in serious violence, and ways to prevent or stop it.

It's not easy for any of us to admit that our children are victims of bullying. It's even harder for many of us to learn that our own child could be responsible for intimidating others. But it is our duty as the protectors and nurturers of our children to uncover incidents of bullying—on the Internet or otherwise—and to work together to stop them.

NINE

New Rules Need to Be Made for Cyberbullying

Jonathan Turley

> The following essay was written in response to a case in which parents posed as a boy on MySpace and harassed a local teenage girl. The girl eventually became so distraught by the harassment that she killed herself. The issues raised by the case alarmed Jonathan Turley, a law professor at George Washington Law School, who notes that parents of the girl have no clear way to hold the other parents legally responsible. "Although there is a new law passed by the last Congress criminalizing the use of the Internet to 'annoy,' it is a poorly written statute that is extremely likely to be challenged on constitutional grounds," he writes. Turley argues that new laws need to be created to address cyberbullying.

When Megan Meier logged on to MySpace a little over a year ago [in 2006], she was seeking a new start with new friends. She'd had some hard times: She considered herself overweight, had been bullied in school and had low self-esteem.

Still, things seemed to be getting better. She had just started eighth grade at a new school in Dardenne Prairie, Mo., had lost 20 pounds and made some new friends. Her parents had recently restored her Internet access. (She had lost that privilege when she and a friend had created a secret MySpace page.)

Shortly after getting her access back, Megan was contacted on MySpace by a boy named Josh Evans. He said that he was 16, that he was home-schooled and that he recently had moved to nearby O'Fallon. He was a dream: He played the guitar and drums; he was handsome; and he told Megan that he liked her a lot.

Josh went into detail about his own difficult life and immediately struck a chord with Megan. For six weeks they corresponded. Then, when her infatuation was at its peak, Megan received a well-planned, well-timed blow. Josh suddenly told her, "I don't know if I want to be friends with you any longer because I heard you're not a very nice friend."

Josh then apparently passed her messages on to others, unleashing a torrent of insults from others in an Internet pile-on. She was called fat and a slut. However, according to her father, the last message from Josh was the worst: "Everybody in O'Fallon knows how you are. You are a bad person and everybody hates you. Have a s----y rest of your life. The world would be a better place without you."

Megan fell apart. She went to her room, tied a cloth belt around a support beam in her closet and hanged herself.

Perhaps the only shock that could rival Megan's death was the news (given to her parents by a neighbor) that Josh had never existed—he had been created by adults who lived nearby. These neighbors, supposed friends of the Meier family, had apparently laid the trap in retaliation for Megan's treatment of their own daughter, the girl who had created the secret MySpace page with Megan.

Megan is only the latest victim of cyber-bullying. In Florida, Jeff Johnston, 15, hanged himself by his book-bag strap in 2005, and in Vermont, Ryan Halligan, 13, hanged himself in 2003—both victims of Internet harassment.

There are many disturbing aspects of this story, but two are of particular concern to a lawyer. First, Tina and Ron Meier were told that they had no clear legal recourse—either criminal or civil. It is not a crime to be cruel and immature. Although there is a new law passed by the last Congress criminalizing the use of the

Cyberbullying has led to laws aimed at eliminating Internet misuse.

Internet to "annoy," it is a poorly written statute that is extremely likely to be challenged on constitutional grounds. Other well-established charges, such as child endangerment and other predatory crimes, would be hard to prove in this case.

There are civil charges that could conceivably be brought, such as negligence or intentional infliction of emotional distress, but the Meiers are running out of time to file. Although the law generally holds landowners liable for "attractive nuisances" they create that lure kids into dangerous conditions, there is no comparable law on the books for cyber-based lures.

A second disturbing aspect of the case is that the alleged culprits did not even face public scrutiny or stigma for their actions. The local newspaper refused to publish the name of the family responsible for the e-mails out of consideration, it said, for their young daughter. Other news outlets, such as Fox and CNN, fol-

Are You a Cyberbully?

Have you ever:

• Signed on with someone else's screen name to gather information?

• Impersonated someone over IM or online?

• Forwarded a private IM conversation or e-mail without the permission of the other person?

• Posted pictures or information about someone on a Web site without their consent?

• Used information found online to follow, tease, embarrass, or harass someone in person?

lowed suit, running stories that also withheld the names. In other words, simply because they had a child, the alleged perpetrators were given the benefit of anonymity.

The decision to protect the family's identity was particularly strange because they are involved in a pending criminal case against Ron Meier after he allegedly caused about $1,000 damage to their lawn by driving a truck across it in the weeks after Megan's death.

The Meier case is an example of a growing trend on the part of the media toward omitting names or identifying information from the public because of paternalistic concerns.

In one particularly alarming case, the *Washington Post* in 2000 withheld the race of a man who had stabbed an 8-year-old to death in his grandmother's frontyard. Living near the crime scene in Alexandria and worried for our own children, my wife and I searched the newspaper for a description of the killer still at large. We were given the person's height and general description but not his race—because the newspaper generally declines to publish the race of criminal suspects. Thus, we did not know that Gregory Murphy was African American because the *Post* did not want to foster racial stereotypes.

The media also routinely decline to name victims in rape cases, even when the accuser is subsequently discredited. For example, after an investigation cleared the Duke lacrosse players, the media still refused to publish their accuser's name under some twisted protection policy for false victims.

This week [in November 2007]—more than a year after Megan Meier's death—the names of the neighbors were finally disclosed in published accounts. The disclosure was largely the result of pressure from bloggers, who do not feel bound by the rules of mainstream newspapers and networks and who have been meting out their own form of Internet justice. The neighbors are Lori and Curt Drew, according to news reports.

The Drews' daughter was certainly dealt a bad hand by her parents. However, the media puts itself on a slippery slope when it starts to protect accused wrongdoers on behalf of their progeny, offering a free pass for alleged predators who procreate.

It seems clear that the Drews did not want to kill Megan or even hurt her physically. They are not the first to be grotesquely transformed by a new technology that offers easy availability and anonymity to its users. Yet, if cyber-traps are to be deterred, there must be avenues to guarantee both forms of private relief and public record.

Megan never knew the true identity of those who trapped her, but the people of Dardenne Prairie have a right to know.

TEN

Cyberbullying Should Be Treated the Same as Traditional Bullying

Terry Freedman

> Terry Freedman wrote the following essay in response to
> Stop Cyberbullying Day, a cyberbullying awareness day cre-
> ated in 2007 by Internet activist Andy Carvin. Freedman
> argues that Stop Cyberbullying Day is a flawed concept
> because it continues the common practice of distinguish-
> ing cyberbullying from traditional bullying. Such think-
> ing, he argues, leads people to place overly restrictive rules
> on technology and forces rule makers to need to adjust
> rules constantly to accommodate new technologies. A bet-
> ter idea, he suggests, is that schools treat cyberbullying
> as they would ordinary bullying. After all, he points out,
> heavy-breathing phone calls are not considered some sort
> of techno-harassment, but rather just plain harassment.
> Freedman is an information and communication technol-
> ogy consultant based in England.

The 30th March [2007] saw the first ever Stop Cyberbullying Day.

The sentiments are admirable and I cannot imagine any normal person disagreeing with them. But is this the most effective way of removing this modern scourge?

Aggressive text messages are one of the most common forms of cyberbullying. This one reads "I hate you."

I suppose the inspiration for this comes from established events such as, in the UK, National No Smoking Day. From the (little) research I've done, the No Smoking Day raises awareness and gives some people the incentive and the moral support they need to make a last ditch effort to give up the weed.

A Stop Cyberbullying Day Is Ineffective

I have to say that, in the days when I smoked, it was completely ineffective, but even if it had been, is it properly analogous to cyberbullying? I mean, are there really people who will wake up on No Cyberbullying Day (which I assume will become an annual event) and say to themselves, "OK, today's the day that I'm finally gonna quit being an online predator/stalking/posting nasty comments/making and distributing secret films on my cell phone/etc etc"?

And that last sentence is, I think, a summary of what the problem is: smoking is smoking is smoking, but there are all different forms of cyberbullying. More importantly, as far as I am aware nobody gave up smoking because they were concerned about the effects of passive smoking: they gave up for completely selfish reasons. So, why should I, as a cyberbully, give up cyberbullying? I mean, what's in it for me?

I do have more fundamental criticisms, but please regard this as thinking aloud.

Do Not Distinguish Between Cyberbullying and Ordinary Bullying

To start with, is it completely legitimate to distinguish between cyberbullying and "ordinary" bullying? Cyberbullying is a function of the technology, but what we ought to be concerned with is behaviour. By focusing on the technology, we lay two traps for ourselves:

First, we will be constantly attempting to update our definition of cyberbullying, which is a pointless task in my opinion. After all, heavy breathing phone calls are a form of techno-bullying, but we don't call it that. We call it harassment. And there are laws against harassment.

Second, and more important in a way, aren't we merely drawing attention to the nastier aspects of technology, and in so doing giving the green light to those whose "solution" is to ban everything (in school)?

Next, given that any type of bullying is about behaviour, it seems to me that there are two ways of tackling it. One is to have an anti-bullying policy that is a policy in the sense that it's written down and there are posters all over the place saying "No bullying". The other is to really have a policy.

How Schools Should Handle Cyberbullying

For there to be a real policy, it has to be embedded in the very fabric of the institution, be that a school, place of work or even a website. Let's see what that might mean in a school situation:

1. Bullying is not done by the Headteacher [the most senior teacher in a British school] or Principal et al to the rest of the staff.
2. Staff don't bully the children. The point is, children learn from the hidden curriculum, which means they go more by what we do than by what we say. I don't know what the situation is like in other parts of the world, but workplace bullying is an unfortunate fact of life in modern Britain, and my impression is that it's getting worse. That isn't setting much of an example to our kids.
3. The school punishes or at least deals with the bullies. What does that mean in terms of cyberbullying?
4. The school provides victims with support. So, what can we do to support victims of cyberbullying? I would suggest that we make people (teachers and parents, as well as kids) aware of the resources that already exist to tackle the problem of bullying in general as well as "specialist" forms such as cell phone bullying. . . .
5. In England, we have a policy called Every Child Matters. This has 5 outcomes which schools and Local Authorities must achieve vis-a-vis each child, and one of these is that the child must feel safe. In my book *Every Child Matters: What It Means For The ICT Teacher* I give practical examples of how issues like safety can be addressed by teachers of educational technology. The point of saying that is not to make you rush out and buy the book (although I won't object if you do), but to point out that a more effective way of tackling cyber (or any other kind of) bullying would be, in my opinion, to encourage teachers to come up with ways in which they can address it as part of what they do in the classroom, both on a behavioural level and in terms of the subject matter.

Every School Should Set a Clear Behavior Policy

6. Schools should not have an internet acceptable use policy: they should have an acceptable behaviour policy. Period. And the simpler and shorter, the better.

Cyberbullying Victims by Grade Level

"I have received mean or threatening e-mail or other messages."

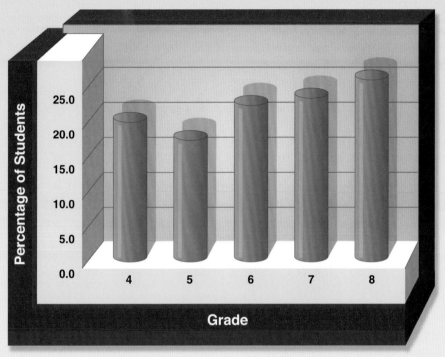

Taken from: i-SAFE America, 2004.

7. By the same token, schools should not have an e-safety officer, which causes people to focus on the technology and therefore come up with the same old hackneyed excuse for doing nothing, ie "I don't understand how this works." Schools already have (at least, they do in the UK), a child protection officer, and it's that person who should be given overall responsibility for countering bullying, including cyberbullying, and not the technology co-ordinator. Like I said at the start, this is a behavioural, not a technological, issue.

8. Raise staff, parental and child awareness by organising in-school talks by the police and other agencies. Sometimes they can bring matters right down to earth. Last year [2006], at the launch of *Safeguarding Children in a Digital World*, on which I'd

been employed as a consultant, a police officer gave a talk in which he said something along the lines of:

> A lot of people regard it as a joke that some men expose themselves on the internet; they regard it as not nice but harmless. So I ask them: would you employ such a person as a babysitter for your own kids? Because if, like me, your answer is "no", it means that you agree that it shouldn't be tolerated.

9. I think ultimately that that's what it comes down to: is bullying of any kind tolerated by a school, or is [it] proactively tackled? Proactively tackled, not just reactively tackled.

10. By the same token, do we allow bullying on our blogs? I personally have a policy that if anyone makes a comment on one of my posts in which they swear, I won't publish it. Not because it bothers me, but because I don't see why it should be the case that someone exploring my website be confronted with some real nastiness. That is my way of not tolerating that kind of behaviour. And to anyone who bleats to me about freedom of speech, I say that these people can express themselves how they like, but not on my patch!

I am not totally dismissing the No Cyberbullying Day. At least someone (Andy Carvin) did something. It has certainly got a debate going, and anti-bullying resources are already starting to be referenced through it. But my point is, unless bullying *per se* is tackled at a much more practical level, this campaign will come to be little more than a way of making ourselves feel good about tackling a problem without actually doing very much about it.

ELEVEN

Hazing Needs to Stop

Jana Lunceford

In the following selection Jana Lunceford details some of the low points in the history of fraternity and sorority hazing. She wrote the piece as a plea to Greek organizations to stop such violent practices. Lunceford, who did not pledge to join a sorority, can understand the appeal of joining an organization that promises friendship and loyalty but does not understand why joining needs to include hazing. "Hazing is an issue that needs to be reviewed and reevaluated," she writes. Lunceford wrote this as the opinion editor of the *Vanguard*, the student newspaper for the University of South Alabama.

With all the talk of hazing happening these days, I can't help but wonder what really goes on behind fraternity and sorority doors at the University of South Alabama. I myself have never been involved in a Greek social club during my college years, and therefore I can't fairly rip any organization a new one. However, in search of finding the truth behind hazing and other rituals practiced by fraternities and sororities around the country, I came across some astounding and noteworthy information concerning the morals behind these organizations.

Jana Lunceford, "Hazing Still Remains a Disturbing Truth," *The Vanguard*, February 6, 2006. Reproduced by permission.

While hazing has been being practiced since the early eighteenth century, I have yet to find one case where the vicious types of hazing were worth being passed down through the centuries or even allowed to evolve over the years. From simply making a pledge run around naked in nothing but his socks, to sodomizing others with household cleaning items, hazing is an issue that needs to be reviewed and re-evaluated.

Take for instance the case of 19-year-old fraternity pledge, Chad Saucier. Growing up in Mobile and attending a local community college, Chad was allowed to pledge Phi Delta Theta, a fraternity at Auburn University. While going through the pledge process, Chad was beat on more than one occasion with a paddle that caused back injuries. One night at a big party, sources say Chad was encouraged to drink large amounts of alcohol. Later that night Chad passed out, choked on his own vomit and died. Here is the sad thing. His so called "brothers" left him in a room, in a ridiculous elf costume required to be worn at the party, and did nothing that would even be recognized as taking care of an obviously sick man.

Hazing Happens in Sororities, Too

While this is the story of several fraternity hazing deaths, sororities too are not out of the loop. On Sept. 9, 2002, Kristen High and Kenitha Saafir were drug by Kappa Alpha Kappa sisters to the beach where they were to perform initiation rituals. The women were blindfolded, bound together at the hands and led out into the ocean where six-foot waves were breaking. The two women were unable to beat the strong force of rip currents and drowned. At the time of the incident, the sorority declined any comments concerning the girls' death and didn't even attempt to contact the deceased families to offer even simple condolences.

The most grotesque and sickening incident of hazing can be found not in a college Greek organization, but yet a high school football team. In Long Island, N.Y., three high school football players were sodomized with a broomstick, golf balls and pine cones covered in a substance similar to Icy Hot. The freshmen were forced to keep quiet about the incident, but when one of the victims required medical attention, all three came clean. The 16-year-old linebacker was initially named responsible for committing the horrendous act.

With all these [instances] in mind, I can only hope that similar practices aren't even thought of on the campus of South Alabama. Even so-called harmless acts such as taking a marker and marking the "flaws" of fellow sorority sisters are degrading and pointless. Does it make any sense to pay money to be part of an organization

Pallbearers carry the casket of a young woman who died while taking part in a sorority hazing activity.

Types of Hazing Experienced by Students at Cornell University

Hazing Experience	Percentage of Students
• Participating in drinking contest/games	17
• Being deprived of sleep	15
• Carrying around unnecessary objects or items	14
• Being required to remain silent or being silenced	13
• Being yelled, cursed, or sworn at	10
• Having food thrown at you or other new members	6
• Being kidnapped or transported and abandoned	5
• Acting as a personal servant to others	5
• Being pressured to eat something you didn't want	5
• Associating with specific people, not others	4
• Destroying or stealing property	4
• Being tied, taped up, or confined	3
• Engaging in or simulating sexual acts	2
• Being hit, kicked, or physically assaulted in some form	1
• Making body alterations (branding, tattooing, piercing)	<1

Taken from: Shelly Camp, PhD, Gretchen Paulos, John W. Sipple, PhD, "Prevalance and Profiling: Hazing Among College . . . Students and Points of Intervention," *American Journal of Health Behavior*, March–April 2005, pp. 137–149.

that points out your freshman fifteen when God only knows they have a four year supply of cottage cheese resting on their hump?

Could you imagine forcing your fellow fraternity brothers to drink obscene amounts of alcohol until they passed out? And when they didn't wake up, tossing them aside like nothing ever happened?

Why Do Pledges Participate?

Yes, I know what many of you are thinking. Why did these victims even participate? Didn't they have a brain of their own? Well, yes they did. But they also have a heart, and a need to be loved just like everyone else. Fraternities and sororities base their existence on the bonds of brotherhood and sisterhood. The appeal of having a group of people claiming to have your back, as long as you pledge your loyalty, is surely an aspect that would draw in anyone looking for a friend.

I drive down Greek Row and only hope that initiation requirements are no worse than a butt whooping your mama laid on you when you were eight. And I can only hold faith that the rushes, pledges and members of each organization have enough dignity and integrity not to physically, emotionally, or spiritually enforce or subject themselves to the harsh practices a lesser organizations participates [in]. Lastly, I hope that should any morally degrading ritual be practiced, that the deaths of the aforementioned would serve as a reminder of what happens when sheer stupidity is set in motion. I hope the Greek organizations will be remembered by the letters they represent, and not the letters on a fellow member's grave.

TWELVE

It Is Futile to Try to Stop Hazing

Bryan Yang

> Bryan Yang is neither a fraternity member nor a fan of hazing. "Hazing is ridiculous," he writes, adding that the whole idea of it is "a bizarre notion." Yet he argues that it is futile to try to stop the practice. He points out that victims agree to their victimization and once hazing is over, they rarely will talk about the practice to others. Trying to stop hazing, he argues, often pushes it further underground, where school officials have a more difficult time monitoring it. Yang's suggestion is that schools leave fraternities alone but keep an eye on hazing to make sure that it does not get too out of hand. Yang wrote this editorial for the *Orion*, the student newspaper for California State University, Chico.

No one can stop Greek [fraternity] hazing. Not Chico State, not the police, not new laws. Nothing and no one can end hazing. It will always be a problem, and it will always exist. Hazing just won't go away, and there is no remedy that will make it completely disappear. It's a lot like herpes.

Hazing is ridiculous. Humiliating oneself in front of people to become accepted is a bizarre notion, but people see it as a rite of passage. Having a good personality and being a nice person doesn't get you too far these days. You have to be bound, gagged,

Bryan Yang, "Hazing Horrible, But It Won't Go Away," *The Orion*, December 6, 2006. Reproduced by permission.

dropped at the outskirts of town and be forced to find your way back home to prove your friendship. Everyone knows that people who are willing to do that to you will be the best of bros.

Trying to stop hazing is unproductive. The authorities don't have the manpower to catch the sheer number of Greeks who participate in hazing rituals. It would be nearly impossible to catch and stop all of those who haze.

Many Greek activities are shrouded in secrecy, which makes the acts difficult to prevent. Greeks will not tell anyone about their sacred rituals. One would have an easier time getting a straight answer from President [George W.] Bush regarding whether Iraq is in a civil war.

Victims Will Not Tell

A good friend of mine pledged a sorority at Sacramento State, a university not known for excessive partying or dangerous hazing. She would not even tell me what hazing rituals she had to go through. Even though she assured me the hazing was not bad, she still adhered to her vow to never tell a word of what went on.

Warning Signs of Hazing

- Group members justifying an activity by saying "it's tradition"

- The presence of alcohol

- Secrecy

- Peer pressure for everyone to participate

- Singling out an individual or specific group

Taken from: Arizona Student Unions, The University of Arizona.

If Greeks aren't willing to come forward and tell people what sorts of painless hazing they go through, they surely won't tell people about some of the more sadistic rituals. That is what makes investigating hazing so difficult.

Hazing is a victimless crime. The only people who are appalled by hazing are usually those on the outside looking in. The parents, professors and students are usually the ones who take the most offense toward hazing. The ones actually hazed

Five girls were injured during a brutal hazing at Glenbrook North High School, in Northbrook, Illinois, in 2003.

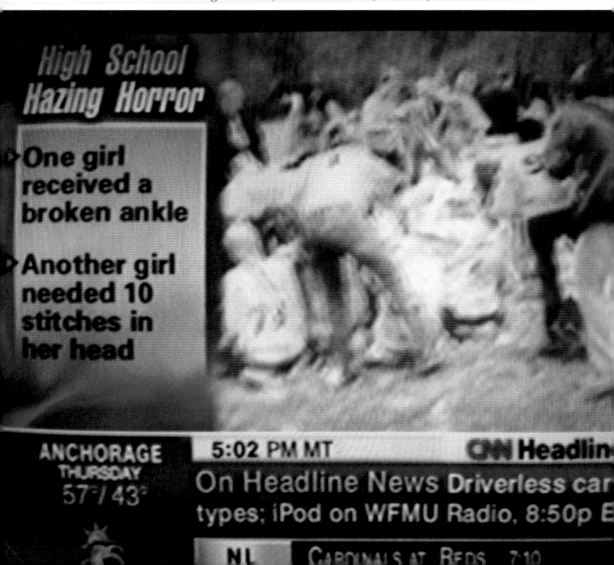

hardly ever press charges and just subject themselves to the hazing process.

You rarely hear the person getting hazed saying, "Hey guys, can we go about this hazing another way? I feel that doing numerous jumping jacks while you electrocute my genitals and force me to drink gallons of curdled milk is a bad idea. I think I could possibly get hurt."

And you rarely hear the reply, "Well, we never thought of it like that. I see the point you're making, friend. We'll settle this in a game of Yahtzee instead. If you win, you're in. Golly gee, if you lose, you're in, too. Hazing is a bad idea. I'm glad you set our unrecognized fraternity straight. Someone could have gotten hurt pretty badly."

Punishments Do Not Work

Hazing doesn't stop because the punishments for it are absurd. First-year students can now only rush in the spring term. This doesn't stop a single thing. It just puts off the inevitable.

After Matthew Carrington's death in 2005, Chico State President Paul Zingg threatened to ban all fraternities and sororities. Carrington was a 21-year-old Chico State student pledging the unrecognized Chi Tau fraternity when he died of water intoxication in the fraternity's basement Feb. 2, 2005. He had been doing calisthenics and drinking water from a 5-gallon jug throughout the night, police said.

Simply getting rid of university recognition could possibly be the least effective punishment. This would cause a rampant surge in the number of unrecognized fraternities and sororities that have no rules and no one to answer to. At least the recognized Greeks now feel obligated to do some charity to be a positive part of the community.

Hazing cannot be stopped. Let the Greeks do what they want, so long as they aren't killing pledges left and right. Their hazing rituals are insulting and humiliating, but let them continue. The participants know full well what they are getting into once they rush. The school and the police have bigger worries than fraternities tying bricks to pledges' man-meat. Let them build their strange brotherhoods and sisterhoods through ridiculous shenanigans. Keep an eye on them, and punish them harshly if they commit serious crimes.

THIRTEEN

Sports Hazing Is Becoming a Bigger Problem

Tom Weir

In the following article Tom Weir writes that a rise in vicious sports-hazing incidents are taking school officials by surprise. Weir cites an Alfred University study that found that about half of hazing victims are athletes. Norman Pollard, who coauthored the study, says, "It gets a little worse each year, until it gets to the breaking point." Oddly, many students do not recognize hazing when it happens, thinking that hazing activities are just "fun" or "fitting-in processes." But hazing can have devastating effects, including depression, suicide, and retaliation. Weir is a sports writer for *USA Today*.

Soccer players who had their heads forced into toilets weren't the only ones shocked when a hazing ritual took on a sadistic edge this year [2003] at Woodridge High School in Peninsula, Ohio.

"It was going on right under our noses, for a few years anyway, and we had no idea," says Jerry Graham, Woodridge's school district superintendent.

Graham is among many high school administrators across the USA who are perplexed by escalating violence associated with hazing. Researchers at Alfred (N.Y.) University, in the first study of its kind, say about 1.5 million high school students are hazed each year, and about half of those victims are athletes, the group facing the greatest risk of enduring these often-dangerous initiations.

Teammates Perpetuate Hazing

"One of the things we find is that the teammates who perpetrate the hazing are the ones who suffered it the year before, and they want to make it that much more dangerous, to validate their experience," says Norman Pollard, Alfred's director of counseling/student development.

Pollard led studies in 1999, asking college students about their hazing experiences in high school, and in 2000, directly surveying high school students on hazing. He continues to research the issue. "It gets a little worse each year," Pollard says, "until it gets to the breaking point."

Hazing Is Getting More Violent

Among recent incidents:

- After the football team at Mepham High School in Bellmore, N.Y., held a training camp last summer [2003] in Pennsylvania, older players were charged with sodomizing younger players with broom sticks, pine cones and golf balls. The football season was canceled, the coaching staff was fired and three players face criminal charges. A judge has determined whether the players should be tried as adults, but the ruling has been sealed.

- A "powder puff" football game between senior and junior girls at Glenbrook North High in suburban Chicago this year [2003] degenerated into a melee that left five juniors seeking medical treatment. The school district expelled 33 seniors and disciplined 20 juniors. Sixteen teens were convicted of misdemeanor battery or alcohol charges.

- In the last year, similar allegations have been made in virtually every corner of the nation. From the South Dakota town of Spearfish, to Salt Lake City, to Donaldsonville, La., there have been accusations of students being showered with mixtures of urine and vomit, being brutally paddled or being sodomized.

Top coaches agree the climate has changed and little tolerance remains for hazing rituals.

"When I was growing up in the '70s, I guess you could say we were hazed," says Dan Burke, coach of the Palm Bay (Fla.) football team. "They would grab the sophomores and smack them in the belly until it turned red. That was a different time."

The Oklahoma Ruf/Neks, a spirit group associated with Sooner athletics, was disciplined by the university for allegedly hazing pledges.

Adds Bill Blankenship, football coach of Union High in Tulsa: "I was de-pantsed in high school and taped to a goal post in college. It was just something you went through. . . . Those same things wouldn't be acceptable today."

School Officials Are Not Quick to Recognize Hazing

Officials at Alfred University, in western New York, thought they had quelled their hazing problems in the '70s. After a student, Chuck Stenzel, died in 1978 from alcohol poisoning and exposure to cold after being locked in a car trunk during a fraternity hazing, Alfred took steps to ban all forms of hazing.

Stenzel's death helped lead to New York becoming the first of 43 states to enact legislation to make hazing illegal. The laws vary greatly, and Pollard believes they need to be revisited.

But Alfred school officials were stunned in 1998 when intoxicated freshmen football players were seen staggering down a street in a hazing ritual. Some were hospitalized, and an investigation found the players were tied up and forced to drink alcohol until they vomited into a barrel.

"We found out this had been a long-standing tradition," says Pollard, named to head Alfred's hazing studies after university leaders realized there was no definitive research on the issue. About 10,000 athletes at 224 colleges were surveyed about their high school experiences, in conjunction with the NCAA.

One finding: despite only 12% of the athletes saying they had been hazed, 80% said they had been required to participate in dangerous or humiliating activities that fit the description of hazing.

"They thought it was something else," Pollard says. "It was across the board, urban, rural, by sport."

Students Do Not Recognize Hazing Either

That common inability of young people to recognize and define hazing was made clear in a recent USA TODAY interview with five students in Nashville at Glencliff High School. All five were members of the Students Taking a Right Stand (STARS) program and had participated in a "Respect and Protect" campaign aimed at curbing school violence.

Four of the five also said they were unaware of hazing among their peers, aside from gangs. But as they talked about the clubs, teams and groups they belonged to, issues of hazing came to light:

- Senior Kelly Petty, a drum major, said, "When we went to band camp, at this church, the older boys beat the younger boys. They would pull them off the top of the bunk bed and hit them with stuff in pillow cases when they were sleeping." She said that "stuff" included "radios, CD players, anything hard."

- Sophomore Will Gordon said he was forcibly put through a freshman initiation as a football player by six teammates at another high school he had attended. "They tied me to a chair and shaved my head and eyebrows. I saw it as all in fun. We didn't necessarily see it as violence. It was like bonding. No matter what, everybody had it done to them."

- Chris Johnson, a senior, said that on the football team, "When they come to the varsity, we drag them through the mud, stuff like that. If you're good, and you've got potential, we don't do it to you. But if you're no good, we do."

- Brittni Perkins, a junior, said she had gone through "fitting-in processes" to become part of a clique. "I had to do some things—give up my lunch money, or do their homework," she said. "It's something you see every day. It's something you basically have to get over."

Hazing Has Long-Term Consequences

The Alfred University study found about half of college athletes had been hazed in high school, and among those victims, "Many of them talked about being depressed and suicidal," Pollard says. "There were (13%) that said they thought about revenge, and whenever I hear about that I think about [the shootings at] Columbine [High School]."

No studies exist that measure how widespread hazing was in the '60s and '70s, but experts agree it seems to be on the rise. Pollard attributes the perceived increase to changing family dynamics.

"Kids aren't spending a lot of time with adults," Pollard says. "Kids are relying more on teams for stability than they ever have. Not just sports, but any type of team—band, choir—the kids feel it's a privilege to be associated with that team and there needs to be some sort of rite of passage, that you have to earn your right to belong."

When establishing their hazing rituals, Pollard says some teenagers "look to the popular media, to *Fear Factor, Survivor*, those types of shows. . . . I don't think they're the cause (of extreme hazing), but I think in some way it reinforces the behavior."

Adults Need to Get Involved

When classes began this fall [2003] at Bridge Creek High in the suburbs of Oklahoma City, two of the first lectures students heard were from the county sheriff and the district attorney.

"We all delivered the same message, which was that hazing is unacceptable behavior and it will be dealt with," says Bridge Creek Superintendent Terry Brown. "If there's any more of this hazing, there will be charges filed."

Bridge Creek's harder line stems from an incident last spring [2003], when high school baseball players held down and paddled eighth-graders with 1x4 boards in six incidents spread over three days. Two students were suspended and allowed to enter a state-run program where they could get counseling and perform community service instead of facing criminal charges.

"The parents of the kids who did that paddling thought we were too strict," Brown says. "The parents of the kids who were paddled thought we were too easy. To me, that says we were about where we should have been."

Erika Karres, a clinical assistant professor in education at the University of North Carolina and author of *Violence Proof Your Kids Now*, likens some hazing behavior to what she saw perpetrated by Nazis while growing up in Germany during World War II.

"When kids get together, whatever the most negatively creative thought one of them has is, it will be the common denominator,"

Karres says. "If there is one who's already committed violence somewhere else, that kid is going to dominate. It only happens in child and teen circles that the worst dominates the rest. There's never a team that says 'Let's stop it.'"

Hazing Has Many Ramifications

The abuse can have lifelong ramifications, says Ellen deLara, a Syracuse [University] assistant professor of social work, who interviewed about 1,000 hazing victims during research for a book she co-authored, *And Words Can Hurt Forever: How to Protect Adolescents from Bullying, Harassment and Emotional Violence*.

"Just like someone who has been in a war, there can be heightened sensitivities, nightmares, flashbacks," deLara says. "They are carrying around an extreme amount of rage, and that plays out in their relationships. They get triggered by things that seem the slightest bit disrespectful."

DeLara says the most common comment from hazing victims is that "parents don't really have a clue" about the student-generated abuse.

In a Survey of High School Students:

- 95 percent of respondents believe that most people do not report hazing incidents.

- 92 percent of respondents believe that most kids will not report a hazing.

- 59 percent of respondents know about hazing activities.

- 21 percent of respondents state they have been involved in hazing activites.

Taken from: www.insidehazing.com.

She counts herself among the once-naive, and says she was drawn to the issue because "my own children were experiencing some of the issues around bullying and hazing in what I considered to be a very safe community high school" in upstate New York.

And deLara says all students in a school where hazing takes place are affected.

"They have to witness it, hear about it, wonder if it's going to happen to them," she says. "People quit sports teams. It's because they know they're next on the list."

FOURTEEN

Students Keep Hazing a Secret

Julie Ruvolo

> In the following selection Julie Ruvolo writes that most college officials do not know the full extent of campus hazings. Why? Because students do not report them. The lack of information goes in both directions because, in the interest of confidentiality, university officials often do not tell students about the reports they do receive. There is even less reporting on sports hazing, writes Ruvolo, because, in many cases, there is not a specific review process for them. Ruvolo wrote this as a senior at Stanford University.

I was shocked when I saw the "torture photos" taken at Abu Ghraib prison outside of Baghdad. Naïve, I know, but I didn't expect that "our soldiers" would do that. Not because I buy into the ideology that the U.S. is "good" and everyone else is "evil," but because I had faith that the infrastructure of military operations over in Iraq would be accountable.

Silly me. My biggest surprise, however, is that the information ever became public.

Sexual humiliation has a long history at U.S. universities in the form of hazing. Prison torture does not equate to university-level hazing, but they are not without similarities. Sexual humiliation has been the most high-profile type of athletic and Greek

Julie Ruvolo, "The Constant Hush-Hush on College Hazing," *The Stanford Daily*, May 7, 2004. Reproduced by permission.

Percentage of High School Students Who Said They Were Hazed When They Joined a Group

Initiation Rites	Inclusive Percentage
• Hazing of any form	48
• Humiliating hazing	43
• Potentially illegal hazing	29
• Substance abuse hazing	23
• Dangerous hazing	??

Group	Percentage
• Fraternity or sorority	76
• Sports team	35
• Cheerleading squad	34
• Church group	24
• Music, art, or theater group	22
• Newspaper or yearbook	17

Taken from: Nadine C. Hoover, PhD, and Norman J. Pollard, PhD, "Initiation Rites in American High Schools: A National Survey," Alfred University, August 2000. www.alfred.edu/hs_hazing.

hazing in recent years. This is a delicate transition, but work with me.

First, the obvious differences. Greek pledges and new team members are joining a group on their own accord—they're not in prison—and when they cross over to normal member status, they are empowered to do the same . . . to the next generation. Also, sports and Greek hazing is internal: The hazed and the hazers are in the same organization and not from separate, warring countries. And most university-level hazers are not stupid enough to take incriminating photos.

Second, not all hazing is created equal. We hear about the worst cases, like at Mepham High School in Long Island, where a few guys on the football team were sodomized with broomsticks and golf balls in 2003. Or the University of Vermont's hockey team, which had its new members do an "elephant walk" connected by each other's genitals, which resulted (among other things) in its season being cut short and the university paying one hazed player $80,000 in a court settlement. These kinds of incidents are few and far between, but I have to wonder how many incidents never go public.

Hazing Stays "Under the Radar"

What about Stanford? Stanford is the land of petty hazing and confidentiality. A study by Alfred University and the NCAA [National Collegiate Athletic Association] estimated that 80 percent of college athletes are hazed, and I am not surprised, since hazing includes getting wasted. This is the kind of hazing that goes on at Stanford and most of it stays under the radar. My friend freshman year joined a club sport and they had her drink beer out of a shoe. Only she doesn't drink alcohol, so they gave her some soda. She had fun, they had fun, what's the big deal?

Too bad it's not all beer and funny fluorescent costumes. While the Office of Student Affairs [OSA] is investigating incidents of champagne and strawberries in hot tubs, they've missed a big thing or two in the last few years. I know, because all of us students know things the administration doesn't find out about.

The OSA doesn't go out looking for information, but rather processes the information that comes to them. This is part of why most hazing stays under the radar—most of us don't tell on each other. Incidentally, athletic hazing is not handled by the OSA, since sports teams are not registered student organizations, although the set-up is under review. So who the hell knows what happens with athletes?

Students Do Not Tell

Most of us on campus are in the dark about what the administration does discover. The OSA's policy is to keep problems private

College fraternities and sororities have often been criticized for their hazing rituals.

and confidential, except in cases where the student organization goes to the press first. So for the large part, they don't know what we know and we don't know what they know.

Aside from petty hazing (who cares), the more troubling stuff I have heard about in the last four years includes group vomiting, being forced to refrain from your extracurricular commitments, social probation (that means you can't talk to anyone), relocation from your housing, physical beatings and, okay, rumors of forced nudity and anal penetration. But none of this stuff is public knowledge at Stanford. We don't tell on our friends and the administration doesn't tell on our friends. It remains precisely at the level of hearsay.

Most seniors don't even know that a member of our class was hazed to the point of hospitalization our freshman year. His fraternity was severely reprimanded, his pledge class doesn't like him, he never made it in the fraternity anyway and the people who do know about it wonder how the hell you found out.

Is anyone noticing a trend? This is the same campus where I still feel safe walking around alone late at night because we never hear about the sexual assaults and rapes that do go on. It's like a bubble within a bubble. But how can we ask for more disclosure without also expecting crackdowns on the hazing we don't want them to know about, or that no one cares to see punished?

What You Should Know About Bullying and Hazing

Facts About Bullying

- About 30 percent of students report being involved with bullying either as a bully (13 percent), a victim (10.6 percent), or as both a bully and a victim (6.3 percent).
- Although school violence is decreasing, bullying is increasing.
- Approximately 160,000 students avoid school each day for fear of being bullied.
- People who are bullied are at a greater risk for developing depression, anxiety disorder, or violent behavior.
- Gifted children are especially vulnerable to the effects of bullying.
- A study found that children bullied for the first time before they hit puberty seem to get over it fairly easily, but those who are victimized for the first time in puberty are more likely to become more aggressive and to turn to alcohol.
- Bullying is most common from sixth to eighth grade.
- Signs of someone being bullied include: unexplained injuries, suddenly falling grades, lack of interest in activities, physical complaints to stay home from school, missing belongings or lunch money.
- Risk factors for being bullied include: being disabled, being socially isolated, being insecure or unassertive, being unathletic, and being easily upset or quick to cry.
- Bullies are less likely to finish school, get or hold a job, or have a stable relationship by the time they are thirty.

- Sixty percent of boys who were categorized as bullies in sixth grade had been convicted of at least one crime by the age of twenty-four and 40 percent had three or more convictions.

Bullying and Gender

- In general, girls are more likely to be bullied in emotional ways such as being left out of activities. Boys are more likely to be physically bullied and threatened.
- Boys and girls are subjected to teasing and name-calling about equally.
- Boys are less likely to admit being bothered by bullying and, if they do, they say they feel angry about it. Girls are more likely to report feeling sad about it.

Cyberbullying

- Cyberbullying is using technology like cell phone text and photo messages, Web sites, blogs, chat rooms, social networking sites, instant messaging services, and e-mail to make fun of, embarrass, or harass others.
- The most common form of cyberbullying is someone forwarding a private e-mail, IM, or text message.
- Girls are more likely than boys to experience cyberbullying.
- Older girls are the most likely to be bullied online, with 41 percent of girls aged fifteen to seventeen reporting being cyberbullied.
- Almost 40 percent of users of social networks such as Facebook and MySpace have been cyberbullied, as compared with 22 percent of online teens who do not use social networks.
- Only about 41 percent of cyberbullying victims tell someone else about it.
- Even though cyberbullying is on the rise, kids are still more likely to be bullied offline than online.

Hazing

- Students often do not realize that they are being hazed. In one study, one in five students reported being subjected to behavior that met the definition of hazing, but when asked if they had been hazed, only one in twenty said yes.

- Hazing is generally defined as an action by an individual or group of persons that involves physical or emotional endangerment of another individual as a condition or part of membership in an organization or class.
- Common practices for fraternity and sorority hazing include: deprivation of food or sleep, demeaning games, pitting pledges against one another, and sensory deprivation and exhaustion practices.
- In a groundbreaking Alfred University study, one in five college athletes reported being subjected to potentially illegal hazing, including being kidnapped, beaten, tied up, and abandoned. They were also forced to destroy property, make prank phone calls, or harass others.
- Half of college athletes were required to participate in alcohol-related hazing, and two-thirds were subjected to humiliating hazing such as being yelled at; being forced to wear embarrassing clothing; or being deprived of sleep, food, or personal hygiene.
- Only one in five student athletes had only positive initiation activities like team trips.
- Football players were more at risk for the most dangerous and illegal hazing.
- Women are more likely to be involved with alcohol-related hazing than other types.

What You Should Do About Bullying and Hazing

What do bullying and hazing have in common? Both involve people not treating each other kindly. In a general sense, hazing is a form of bullying—one that is condoned by a group or organization. Fighting bullying and hazing can be tricky, since it involves taking a stand against peers and taking a social risk. Luckily, teens can—and have—worked with other students, adults, their schools, and their communities to stop bullying and hazing.

If You Are Being Bullied

For students who are high school age and younger, bullying is the bigger problem. The Web site for the American Academy of Pediatrics recommends that kids who are bullied respond with the "walk, talk, squawk" technique. Walk means walking calmly away from the bully. Walking is better than running, because bullies will interpret running as being scared. Talk means talking calmly and confidently to bullies. And squawk means telling a teacher or a parent about the bullying.

The teen health Web site of the Nemours Foundation recommends the following responses to bullies:

- Ignore the bully and walk away.
- Hold in your anger around the bully.
- Do not get physical.
- Practice confidence.
- Take charge of your life.
- Talk about it.
- Find your (true) friends.

Getting Other People Involved

If bullying is not something you feel like you can handle yourself, there are other things you can do. One is to stick with a friend or group of friends for safety. Avoid places where bullies tend to hang out. Let parents or teachers know about the bullying problem. Often kids are too embarrassed to admit they are being bullied. If you are too embarrassed about your bullying, you could write a note to your parents, teacher, or a school official.

If bullying is a big problem at your school, talk to friends about it and find people who are concerned about it. Join an antiviolence group or, if there is not one, organize one at your school. Speak with school officials or at a PTA meeting and suggest that your school participate in an antiviolence program.

If Your Friend Is Being Bullied

One of the best ways to help a friend who is being bullied is simply to be a good friend to them. Listen to them if they want to talk about the bullying. If they are in a situation in which they might be bullied, make sure to walk with them. Try to find a different, bully-free route to take. Encourage your friend to tell an adult about the bullying, and if they are too afraid, tell someone on their behalf. Make sure your friend knows that the bullying is not their fault. If your friend shows any signs of being extremely upset or suicidal about the situation, tell an adult right away, even if your friend does not want you to.

If You Are the Bully

It is not easy to admit to being a bully, but once you do, you can work on stopping your behavior. The Girls' Health Web site of the U.S. Department of Health and Human Services recommends the following steps:

- Recognize and admit that you are a bully and acknowledge that your actions are hurting others.
- Talk to an adult that you can trust.
- Look within yourself to find better ways to deal with anger.

- Form healthy relationship with kids your own age.
- Put yourself in the other person's shoes.
- Make a change and be friendly to others.

Hazing

For people in college, hazing becomes more of a concern. One of the biggest obstacles to stopping hazing is that often people do not realize that what is going on is hazing—and possibly illegal as well. What might seem like harmless fun or just silly could be a form of hazing. The first step to stop hazing is to realize what hazing is. The University of Michigan's Web site offers some questions to ask yourself to determine if hazing is happening. Would you let a *New York Times* reporter see and report what you are doing? Would you tell prospective members what they will go through? Would all the parents and family members of your organization be welcome during the activity? Would you allow the president of the university, the dean of students, or your coach to be present at this event? Would you allow interested members of the police department to witness your event?

If It Is Hazing

People go along with hazing for many reasons. Some think it is a time-honored tradition. Others think it fosters bonding. Some think it is just something that must be endured. And others are simply too scared to speak out.

Hazing is not going to stop unless people start speaking out against it. Talk informally with people in your pledge class or on your team to gauge what their feelings are on hazing. Often only a few people really want to keep hazing, and the rest are just going along with it. If you discover a lot of antihazing sentiment, you could consider refusing, as a group, to go through with hazing activities.

Alternatives to Hazing

There are plenty of ways to foster team building and friendship without humiliating or hurting other group members. StopHazing.

org, an organization with the goal of eliminating hazing, offers these ten alternatives to traditional hazing:

- Foster unity: Pledges can work together on a project or a challenge, such as a ropes course.
- Develop problem-solving abilities: Pledges can work together on solving problems with the chapter.
- Develop leadership skills: Pledges can work as mentors, in leadership positions, and learn from leaders in the community.
- Instill a sense of membership: Plan special events for the whole chapter to attend.
- Promote scholarship: Place an emphasis on academic achievement.
- Build awareness of chapter history: This can include inviting older alumni to speak about the chapter's early history.
- Knowledge of the Greek system: Find leaders who will come and talk about the fraternity and sorority systems.
- Aid career goals: Encourage pledges to take advantage of the career-building program offered by the school.
- Involve pledges in the community: Have pledges get involved with community service projects.
- Improve relations with other fraternity and sorority systems: Have pledges work together on projects with pledges from other houses.

If hazing seems like too big a problem to handle alone, you can also alert adults involved with the organization, such as a coach or university officials, as to what is going on. If you do not feel comfortable doing that or fear negative consequences, you can alert an official anonymously.

The editors have compiled the following list of organizations concerned with the issues debated in this book. The descriptions are derived from materials provided by the organizations. All have publications or information available for interested readers. The list was compiled on the date of publication of the present volume; the information provided here may change. Be aware that many organizations take several weeks or longer to respond to inquiries, so allow as much time as possible.

Center for Safe and Responsible Internet Use (CSRIU)
474 W. Twenty-ninth Ave., Eugene, OR 97405
(541) 344-9125 • fax: (541) 344-1481
e-mail: info@csriu.org • Web site: www.cyberbully.org

CSRIU provides research and outreach services to address issues of the safe and responsible use of the Internet. They provide guidance to parents, educators, librarians, policy makers, and others regarding effective strategies to assist young people in gaining the knowledge, skills, motivation, and self-control to use the Internet and other information technologies in a safe and responsible manner.

Coalition for Children
PO Box 6304, Denver, CO 80206
(303) 809-9001 • fax: (303) 320-6328
e-mail: kraizer@safechild.org • Web site: www.safechild.org

Coalition for Children seeks to protect children from bullying and sexual, emotional, and physical abuse. They provide teacher training, parent education, and community awareness to implement prevention programs, advocate for children and families, and provide expert witness services and curriculum development services.

Creating Caring Communities (CCC)
6795 E. Tennessee Ave., Ste. 425, Denver, CO 80224
(720) 941-0700 • e-mail: info@creatingcaringcommunities.org
Web site: www.creatingcaringcommunities.com

CCC's mission statement is: "We create safe and caring communities for children and youth." The organization offers training for schools and communities on creating safe and bully-free schools. They are the creators of the training program Bully-Proofing Your School, in which adults and students work together to create a safe school environment.

Kids Against Bullying
8161 Normandale Blvd., Bloomington, MN 55437
(952) 838-9000 • toll-free: (800) 537-2237 • fax: (952) 838-0199
e-mail: bullying411@pacer.org • Web site: www.pacerkidsagainst
bullying.org

Kids Against Bullying is run by the PACER Center, an organization that advocates on behalf of people with disabilities. They offer antibullying programs and resources and sponsor National Bullying Awareness Week.

Mothers Against School Hazing (MASH)
PO Box 14121, Baton Rouge, LA 70898
e-mail: ksavoy@mashinc.org • Web site: www.mashinc.org

The mission of MASH is to eliminate hazing, bullying, and/ or abusive acts toward children through education, communication, and legislation. Their Web site offers antihazing links and resources. They provide speakers and offer a free monthly newsletter.

National Youth Violence Prevention Resource Center (NYVPRC)
600 Clifton Rd., Atlanta, GA 30333
(404) 498-1515 • toll-free: (800) 311-3435 • Web site: www.safe
youth.org

The mission of the NYVPRC is to provide resources that facilitate youth violence prevention. Their Web site offers links, articles, and crisis hotlines for youth issues such as alcohol, bullying, and depression.

North-American Interfraternity Conference (NIC)
3901 W. Eighty-sixth St., Ste. 390, Indianapolis, IN 46268-1791
(317) 872-1112 • fax: (317) 872-1134 • e-mail: nic@nicindy.org
Web site: www.nicindy.org/

The NIC advocates the needs of its member fraternities through advancement and growth of the fraternity community and enhancement of the educational mission of the host institutions. The NIC is also committed to enhancing the benefits of fraternity membership. The NIC has seventy-one member organizations, with approximately fifty-five hundred chapters located on more than eight hundred campuses in the United States and Canada, and approximately 350,000 undergraduate members.

Operation Respect
2 Penn Plaza, Sixth Fl., New York, NY 10121
(212) 904-5243 • e-mail: info@operationrespect.org • Web site: www.dontlaugh.org

Operation Respect's mission is: "To assure each child and youth a respectful, safe and compassionate climate of learning where their academic, social and emotional development can take place free of bullying, ridicule and violence." Operation Respect developed the Don't Laugh at Me (DLAM) programs, which utilize music and video along with curriculum guides based on the well-tested conflict resolution curricula developed by the Resolving Conflict Creatively Program (RCCP) of Educators for Social Responsibility (ESR).

Stop Bullying Now
409 N. Wayne Rd., Wayne, ME 04284
e-mail: stanstopbullyingnow.com • Web site: www.stopbullying now.com

Stop Bullying Now offers antibullying information, research, training, and seminars for teachers and students. It runs Stopbullying. now.com, a Web site that offers information on bullies, including support for bullies and those who are bullied. Stan Davis, the organization's founder, has published several books on bullying, including *Empowering Bystanders in Bullying Prevention*.

Stop Bullying Now!
200 Independence Ave. SW, Washington, DC 20201
toll-free: (877) 464-4772 • e-mail: comments@hrsa.gov • Web site: www.stopbullyingnow.hrsa.gov

Stop Bullying Now! is part of the "Take a stand! Lend a hand!" antibullying campaign run by the U.S. Department of Health and Human Services. Their Web site offers resources for adults and children on preventing and reducing bullying. They also produce antibullying resources, including brochures, posters, and public service announcements.

StopHazing.org
e-mail: info@stophazing.org • Web site: www.stophazing.org

The mission of StopHazing.org is to provide up-to-date information and resources for students, parents, and educators on hazing. Its Web site offers articles, discussion groups, and information on working to stop hazing.

Books

Jodee Blanco, *Please Stop Laughing at Me*. Avon, MA: Adams Media, 2003.

José Bolton Sr. and Stan Graeve, eds. *No Room for Bullies: From the Classroom to Cyberspace, Teaching Respect, Stopping Abuse and Rewarding Kindness*. Boys Town, NE: Boys Town, 2005.

Ellen deLara and James Garbarino, *And Words Can Hurt Forever: How to Protect Adolescents from Bullying, Harassment and Emotional Violence*. New York: Free Press, 2003.

Ricky L. Jones, *Black Haze: Violence, Sacrifice, and Manhood in Black Greek Letter Fraternities*. Albany: State University of New York Press, 2004.

Erika V. Shearin Karres, *Mean Chicks, Cliques and Dirty Tricks: A Real Girl's Guide to Getting Through the Day with Smarts and Style*. Cincinnati: Adams Media, 2004.

Susan Lipkins, *Preventing Hazing: How Parents, Teachers and Coaches Can Stop the Violence, Harassment and Humiliation*. San Francisco: Jossey-Bass, 2006.

Hank Newar, *The Hazing Reader*. Bloomington: Indiana University Press, 2004.

———, *Wrongs of Passage: Fraternities, Sororities, Hazing and Binge Drinking*. Bloomington: Indiana University Press, 2002.

Dickon Pownall-Gray, *Surviving Bullies Workbook: Skills to Help Protect You from Bullying*. Morrisville, NC: Lulu, 2006.

Deborah Prothrow-Stith, Howard R. Spivak, and Janet Reno, *Sugar and Spice and No Longer Nice: How We Can Stop Girls' Violence*. San Francisco: Jossey-Bass, 2006.

Rachel Simmons, *Odd Girl Out: The Hidden Culture of Aggression in Girls*. New York: Harvest, 2003.

Nancy E. Willard, *Cyberbullying and Cyberthreats: Responding to the Challenge of Online Social Aggression, Threats and Distress.* Champaign, IL: Research, 2007.

————, *Cyber-Safe Kids, Cyber-Savvy Teens: Helping Young People to Use the Internet Safely and Responsibly.* San Francisco: Jossey-Bass, 2007.

Periodicals

Anushka Asthana, "Crackdown on Schoolgirl Bullying Epidemic," *Observer* (London), January 20, 2008.

Michelle Bonebrake, "Name Three Qualities to Attract Bullies," *Festus* (MO) *News Democrat Journal,* October 23, 2007.

Norman Draper, "School Has New Plan to Tackle Bullies," *Minneapolis Star Tribune,* January 18, 2008.

Nick Feldman, "Sensitivity Toward Hazing Is Leading to Change, If Only Slowly," *Daily of the University of Washington,* January 17, 2008.

Dani King, "New Traditiation Rules Mean Bummed Alums," *Whitworthian,* September, 18, 2007.

Jen McCoy, "Cyber-Bullying: Changing the Rules for Bullies," *Portage* (WI) *Daily Register,* February 4, 2008.

Katie Menzer, "Boy Scouts Tackle Anti-bullying Tactics," *Dallas Morning News,* January 20, 2008.

Helen Phillips, "Effects of Bullying Worse for Teens," *New Scientist,* October 29, 2004.

Carrie Watters, "Dealing with Girls Who Bully: Social Savvy Used as Power," *Arizona Republic,* February 26, 2006.

Amanda M. Wimmer, "Anti-bullying Lesson Paying Off at South Park," *Oshkosh* (WI) *Northwestern,* January 29, 2008.

Internet Sources

Elizabeth H. Allan and Mary Madden, "Yeah, but It Wasn't Hazing! Research-Based Insights on Why Students Underestimate Hazing," Association of Fraternity Advisors, September 2007. www.stophazing.org/fraternity_hazing/AFA%20Essentials%20 -%20September%202007%20-%20Allan-Madden.pdf.

Allison Bloom, "High School Hazing," TeenWire.com, August 12, 2003. www.teenwire.com/infocus/2003/if-20030812p247-hazing.php.

Robert Brooks, "Hazing: Rituals of Bonding or Humiliation?" DrRobertBrooks.com, April 2004. www.drrobertbrooks.com/writings/articles/0404.html.

Michael Carr-Gregg, "More Action Essential to Curb Bullying," *Australian*, May 16, 2007. www.theaustralian.news.com.au/story/0,20867,217380687583,00.html.

Martina Devlin, "Cyber-Bullying Just an Old Snake in New Skin," *Independent.ie*, August 9, 2007. www.independent.ie/opinion/columnists/martina-devlin/cyberbullying-just-an-old-snake-in-new-skin-1054202.html.

Taunya English, "College Administrators, Students Differ on What Hazing Is," Center for the Advancement of Health, February 28, 2005. http://hbns.org/getDocument.cfm?documentID=1027.

Mayo Clinic Staff, "Bullying: Help Your Child Handle a School Bully," MayoClinic.com, April 24, 2007. www.mayoclinic.com/healt/bullying/MH00126.

Kim Medaris, "Study: Gifted Children Especially Vulnerable to Effects of Bullying," Purdue University, April 6, 2006. http://news.uns.purdue.edu/html4ever/2006/060406.Peterson.bullies.html.

Scott Peitzer, "Hazing Rules Vilify Frats," *Daily Texan*, December 2, 2002. http://media.www.dailytexanonline.com/media/storage/paper410/news/2002/12/02/Opinion/Hazing.Rules.Vilify.Frats-497218.shtml.

Bridie Smith, "Snarl, You're on Bully Camera as Schools Act," *Age*, December 5, 2007. www.theage.com.au/news/national/snarl-youre-on-bully-camera-as-schools-act/2007/12/04/1196530678399.html.

Linda Starr, "Hazing: It's Not Just a College Problem Anymore!" Education World, May 25, 2007.www.education-world.com/a_issues/issues123.shtml.

INDEX

PICTURE CREDITS